RECYCLING AND UPCYCLING

SCIENCE • TECHNOLOGY • ENGINEERING

BY STEVEN OTFINOSKI

CHILDREN'S PRESS®

An Imprint of Scholastic Inc.

CONTENT CONSULTANT
Sherill Baldwin, Environmental Analyst, Connecticut Department of Energy and Environmental Protection

PHOTOGRAPHS ©: cover: Britt Erlanson/Getty Images; 3: Dave and Les Jacobs/Media Bakery; 4 left: The Granger Collection; 4 right: Mike Harrington/Getty Images; 5 left: Monty Rakusen/Media Bakery; 5 right: Media Bakery; 6: Steve Marcus/AP Images; 8: Art Media/The Image Works; 9: Jacob A. Riis/Getty Images; 10 left: F. Gutekunst/Library of Congress; 10 right-11 left, 11 right: The Granger Collection; 12: war posters/Alamy Images; 13: Marty Lederhandler/AP Images; 14 left: Universal History Archive/Getty Images; 14 right-15 bottom: The Keasbury-Gordon Photograph Archive/Alamy Images; 15 top: Joerg Boethling/Alamy Images; 16: Eric Taylor/Getty Images; 17: Andrew Link/AP Images; 18: Mike Harrington/Getty Images; 20: PathDoc/Shutterstock, Inc.; 21: Prisma/Superstock, Inc.; 22 left: Dave and Les Jacobs/Media Bakery; 22 right-23 left: David Leahy/Media Bakery; 23 right: Jim West/Superstock, Inc.; 24: Richard Levine/Alamy Images; 25: Ariel Skelley/Media Bakery; 26 top: Raymond Boyd/Getty Images; 26 bottom: Edwin Remsberg/Alamy Images; 27: Amy Davis/Getty Images; 28: rfletcher/Alamy Images; 29: Brian Vander Brug/Getty Images; 30: imageBROKER/Superstock, Inc.; 32: Hero Images/Media Bakery; 33: Diane Collins/Jordan Hollender/Media Bakery; 34: Kim Karpeles/Alamy Images; 35: Richard B. Levine/Newscom; 38: Monty Rakusen/Media Bakery; 39: Dan Bannister/Media Bakery; 40 left: CB2/ZOB/Newscom; 40 right-41 left: Oli Scarff/Getty Images; 41 right: Steven Siewert/Getty Images; 42: wavebreakmedia/Shutterstock, Inc.; 43: Don Mason/Media Bakery; 44: Media Bakery; 46: Jupiterimages/Media Bakery; 47: Richard B. Levine/Newscom; 48 top: Robert Galbraith/Landov; 48 bottom, 48 top: Justin Sullivan/Getty Images; 48 bottom: Aurora Photos/Alamy Images; 50: David Leahy/Media Bakery; 51: Lourens Smak/Alamy Images; 52 left: Media Bakery; 52 right: B Christopher/Alamy Images; 53: Hero Images/Media Bakery; 54: Monty Rakusen/Media Bakery; 55: Coprid/Shutterstock, Inc.; 56: Rafael Campillo/Superstock, Inc.; 57: Dragan Zivkovic/Alamy Images; 58: PEAT International, Inc./AP Images; 59: Eric Risberg/AP Images.

LIBRARY OF CONGRESS CATALOGING-IN-PUBLICATION DATA
Otfinoski, Steven, author.
 Recycling and upcycling : science, technology, and engineering / by Steven Otfinoski.
  pages cm. — (Calling all innovators: a career for you)
 ISBN 978-0-531-23002-2 (library binding) — ISBN 978-0-531-23220-0 (pbk.)
 1. Environmental sciences — Vocational guidance — Juvenile literature. 2. Recycling (Waste, etc.) — Vocational guidance — Juvenile literature. 3. Salvage (Waste, etc.) — Juvenile literature.
 4. Environmentalists — Juvenile literature. I. Title. II. Series: Calling all innovators.
 GE60.084 2015
 363.72'82 — dc23   2015029119

All rights reserved. Published in 2016 by Children's Press, an imprint of Scholastic Inc.
Printed in the United States of America 113

1 2 3 4 5 6 7 8 9 10 R 25 24 23 22 21 20 19 18 17 16

Science, technology, engineering, the arts, and math are the fields that drive innovation. Whether they are finding ways to make our lives easier or developing the latest entertainment, the people who work in these fields are changing the world for the better. Do you have what it takes to join the ranks of today's greatest innovators? Read on to discover if a career in the exciting world of recycling and upcycling is for you.

TABLE *of* CONTENTS

A street sweeper helps clean up New York City in the late 1800s.

Composting is a great way to reuse food scraps and yard waste.

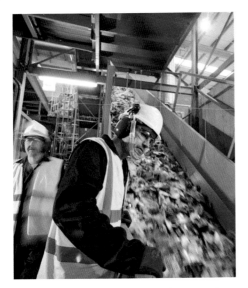

Skilled workers are required to watch over the recycling process.

Plastic bottles are among the many everyday items that can be recycled.

At Apex and other landfills, loaders and bulldozers are used to compact trash. Good compaction reduces odors and rodents.

CHAPTER ONE

CYCLES THROUGH TIME

The largest landfill in the United States lies in a valley just 20 miles (32 kilometers) north of Las Vegas, Nevada. The Apex Landfill contains 59 million tons of trash. This mountain of garbage covers 300 acres (121 hectares) and reaches a peak height of 300 feet (91.4 meters). Opened in 1993, Apex is expected to be used for 250 years. By that time, it will cover more than 2,200 acres (890 ha).

Compared to most of the landfills in America, Apex is well designed and environmentally friendly. An underground plastic lining prevents garbage from polluting the water table and surrounding soil. However, Apex is also a grim reminder of the growing problem of waste management around the world. As landfills fill up, where will we put our trash? How will we stop poisoning our water, land, and air with the things we throw away? The answers to these questions can be summed up in one word—recycling.

LANDMARK LANDFILLS

400 BCE	1937 CE	1974	1993
The world's first **municipal** landfill is established in Athens, Greece.	The Fresno Municipal Sanitary Landfill, the first modern U.S. landfill, opens in California.	Mount Trashmore Park in Virginia Beach, Virginia, opens on the site of an abandoned landfill.	Apex Landfill is established outside Las Vegas, Nevada.

THE EARLY DAYS

People have found ways to conserve and reuse their resources since ancient times. Archaeologists have found recycled glass products in ancient cities such as Sagalassos in what is now Turkey. The ancient Romans melted statues to create new statues or bronze coins. In the Middle Ages, people in Great Britain used ashes from fires as an ingredient in bricks.

"Rag-and-bone men" in the 1800s collected rags, animal bones, and metal products from homes and sold them to small businesses. These businesses used the rags to make papers and ground up the bones for fertilizer. Farmers collected garbage from restaurants to feed their livestock. They used the animals' manure as fertilizer for crops.

A rag-and-bone man walks the streets of Paris, France, in the late 1800s.

BASKET FOR CARRYING RECYCLABLE MATERIALS

In New York City and other large cities, garbage began to pile up in the streets during the 1800s.

THE INDUSTRIAL REVOLUTION

Throughout much of history, manufactured goods in Europe and America were mostly made by hand. This made them expensive. People got the most of their purchases by finding ways to **upcycle** goods for other purposes or recycle them into new products.

This all changed with the Industrial Revolution in the early 1800s. Newly invented machines could turn out products faster and more cheaply than craftspeople working by hand. People bought these goods at a fraction of their former prices. They could afford to dispose of worn-out things and buy new ones. All this garbage soon began piling up. In earlier times, people would bury their own waste. Now, land had to be set aside for **dumps**. Even then, most garbage was tossed into the streets, especially in cities. It mixed with animal and human waste and water. It was unsightly, it smelled bad, and it spread germs and disease. Something had to be done.

PAST MARVELS

George Waring, Jr., knew that cleaner cities would help prevent deadly illnesses.

AMERICA'S FIRST RECYCLING CENTER

Until 1895, New York City, like other American cities, had no organized program for waste management or recycling. That year Colonel George Waring, Jr., a Civil War veteran, was appointed the city's **Sanitation** Commissioner.

FROM MEMPHIS TO NEW YORK

Waring had already had a long career as an engineer and designer of sanitation systems. In 1878, he had created a successful sewer system for Memphis, Tennessee. This helped end a series of yellow fever and cholera **epidemics** that were spread, in part, through the filthy water. In New York, Waring set up a unit of street sweepers who dressed in uniforms and were called the White Wings.

THE APOSTLE OF CLEANLINESS

Waring's plan required New York residents to separate their garbage into bins by type: food waste, ashes from stoves, paper, and street sweepings. In 1897, he set up a recycling center in Manhattan with "picking yards." Here workers would pick through the trash and pull out paper, metal containers, and other things that could be recycled and made into new products. It

A member of the White Wings poses with his broom in 1896.

CART FOR COLLECTING WASTE

WHITE UNIFORM

Street cleaners similar to the White Wings continued working in New York City for many decades.

was the beginning of modern recycling. Waring's efforts in sanitation earned him the title Apostle of Cleanliness.

A TRAGIC END

Waring left New York in 1898 to study waste removal in Cuba. He hoped to bring the success he had in Memphis and New York to yet another location. However, Waring contracted yellow fever, a disease he had helped conquer in Memphis. He died at age 65. ✷

A Gas Mask requires 1.11 pounds of rubber

A Life Raft requires 17 to 100 pounds of rubber

A Scout Car requires 306 pounds of rubber

A Heavy Bomber requires 1,825 pounds of rubber

America needs your SCRAP RUBBER

Posters helped encourage citizens to donate recyclable materials to the war effort during World War II.

A NEED FOR RECYCLING

A serious movement to conserve, reuse, and recycle resources took place during the Great Depression in the 1930s, when millions of people around the world were out of work and had little money. They couldn't afford to buy new things and had to find ways to reuse what they had. They repaired their worn-out products and found creative ways to upcycle items into new uses, such as making clothes from flour sacks.

When the United States entered World War II in 1941, recycling and upcycling became a patriotic duty. The government **rationed** things such as metal and rubber because they were important resources for the military. Many food items were also rationed. In response, people planted "victory gardens" in their yards, growing their own vegetables and fruits. They also used food scraps to create **compost.**

RECYCLING LOST AND FOUND

When the war ended in 1945, America experienced an economic boom. The average person could now afford new products such as cars, stereo systems, and television sets. The country forgot the benefits of recycling as people kept buying new things. Land was cheap, and it was easier for people to toss all their discarded things into municipal dumps and landfills than to recycle.

The 1960s saw great change in these attitudes. People turned their attention to preserving the environment from pollution. By the 1970s, people were rediscovering the importance of recycling as a part of a growing **conservation** movement. By the 1980s, curbside collection of such recyclables as newspapers, metal cans, glass jars, and plastic bottles was becoming a regular part of life across America.

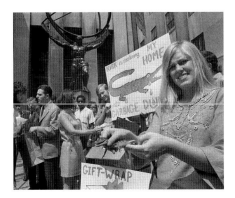

Protecting the environment became a major issue for many people during the 1960s and 1970s.

GARY ANDERSON

The recycling logo that appears on millions of recycling bins and other products was created in 1970 by a 23-year-old student at the University of Southern California. Gary Anderson submitted his design to a competition for a recycling symbol run by the Container Corporation of America. It won out over 500 other entries. Anderson's design was simple and direct. It showed three folded arrows in a continuous cycle, one pointing to the next. The three arrows are meant to represent the three main steps of recycling: the collection of recyclables, the manufacture of new products from them, and the purchase and use of these products. Over the years, Anderson's design has become one of the most recognized logos in the world. It is used to promote recycling everywhere.

VATS OF
RAG PULP

Old rags were bleached and mixed with water to make pulp for paper.

A REVOLUTION IN PAPERMAKING

Newspaper is one of the most recycled materials today. However, paper was once a scarce resource that was commonly made from rags and old clothing. In 1690, at paper mills like the one near Philadelphia (the first to open in America), discarded clothing and rags were beaten into **pulp** and then poured into molds to make paper. But by the 1850s, rags were in short supply, and there was an increasing demand for daily newspapers.

FROM RAGS TO WOOD

Inventors began seeking new ways of making paper. Eventually, they discovered that wood pulp from trees could be transformed into paper with the help of chemicals. In 1868, the first wood pulp sawmill opened in Topsham, Maine. It produced one ton of wood pulp per day. This pulp could be turned into paper cheaply and quickly.

Printers needed plenty of paper to meet the demand for newspapers.

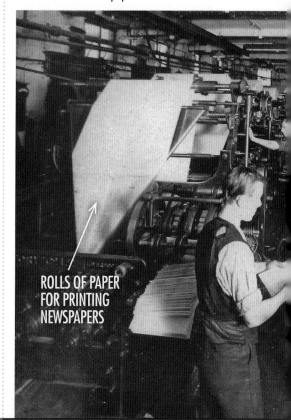

ROLLS OF PAPER
FOR PRINTING
NEWSPAPERS

Piles of wood chips are set aside to be turned into pulp at a mill in Uruguay. Recycling reduces the amount of natural resources used to make new paper and other products.

THE PAPER PROCESS

By the 1930s, almost all paper in the United States was made from wood pulp instead of rags. But while this made paper production easier, it also led to more trees being cut down to make pulp. As people work to conserve trees and other natural resources today, they search for more and more effective ways to turn used paper and cardboard back into pulp. ✳

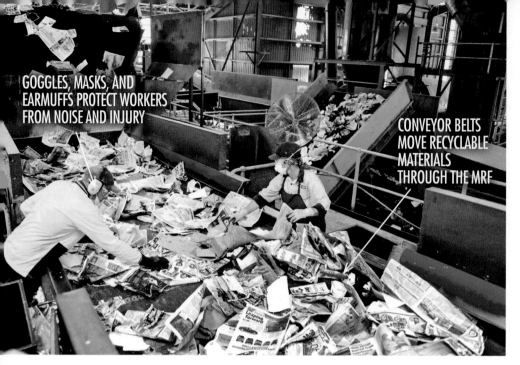

GOGGLES, MASKS, AND EARMUFFS PROTECT WORKERS FROM NOISE AND INJURY

CONVEYOR BELTS MOVE RECYCLABLE MATERIALS THROUGH THE MRF

Workers sort through recyclables at a Materials Recovery Facility.

RECYCLING PAPER AND PLASTIC

From curbside pickup, loose paper, junk mail, and newspapers are taken to either a **transfer station** or Materials Recovery Facility (MRF). They are then bundled to be sold to paper mills. At the mills, the paper is chopped up into tiny pieces and soaked in water and chemicals to be returned to the pulp from which it came. Chemicals remove ink from the paper, and wood fiber is added to strengthen the recycled pulp. The recycled paper is then sold to manufacturers to be made once more into products such as newspapers, books, and cardboard boxes. It is also used in paper products such as paper towels and toilet paper.

Used plastic bottles and jars are collected and delivered to facilities where they are also shredded into tiny pieces. The pieces are heated and treated with chemicals. This transforms them into a thick, sticky liquid. The liquid plastic is then used to create useful products, such as outdoor furniture and carpets.

GLASS AND METAL

Early soda manufacturers had a good way to recycle their product. With the deposit refund system, customers were charged a small deposit of 5 or 10 cents for each bottle purchased. The deposit was fully refunded when the empty glass bottles were returned to the stores. The bottles could then be washed and reused. Today, most large beverage manufacturers have stopped washing the old bottles and reusing them. Instead, the glass is crushed, melted, and formed into new products as part of the recycling process. Some smaller businesses still use refillable bottles because they are so environmentally friendly. But in general, glass bottles have been replaced by plastic bottles.

Since the 1950s, steel and aluminum cans have become popular. Like plastic or glass bottles, they are recyclable. The cans are shredded into pieces and then melted down in a furnace at high temperatures. The liquid metal is cooled and then hardened into blocks. The blocks are pressed flat by machines into thin sheets. These sheets can be shaped into new cans. Aluminum is the most valuable of all recycled materials. In spite of this, Americans throw away about $1 billion worth of aluminum cans each year instead of recycling them.

Bottles must be washed carefully if they are to be filled again.

Composting is a great way to recycle food scraps, yard waste, and other materials instead of throwing them away.

CHAPTER TWO

A WORLD OF RECYCLING

I t's a lovely summer morning in the Hernandez household. After breakfast, Mrs. Hernandez puts the coffee grounds and food scraps in a compost pile in the backyard. This material will later be used to enrich the soil in the family's garden. Her son, Juan, starts his daily chores. This includes vacuuming the new living room carpet that is made entirely of recycled plastic. Amazingly, it looks and feels like any other carpet.

Mr. and Mrs. Hernandez gather up their cloth bags to go food shopping. The bags conserve resources because they are reusable. They won't pollute the environment like the store's plastic bags. Daughter Marie goes outside with her novel, printed on recycled paper, and sits down to read on a lounge chair that is also made entirely of recycled plastic.

Recycling and using recycled products have become a big part of life in the 21st century. The more we recycle, the less waste we throw away that could harm the environment. The great strides we've taken in recycling are making our world a better place to live.

HIGHLIGHTS IN RECYCLING

1897	1968	1973	1976
The first U.S. recycling center is established in New York City.	Aluminum companies begin recycling discarded aluminum cans and other products.	The nation's first curbside recycling program begins in Berkeley, California.	The U.S. government passes the Resource Conservation and Recovery Act to help conserve resources and reduce waste.

FROM COLORED PAPER TO COFFEE CUPS

One-fourth of all garbage is paper, and almost all of this paper is recyclable. Until recently, some kinds of paper products were not recyclable, but new technology is changing that. For example, colored paper once could not be mixed with white paper. Now some paper mills are using a new process to remove colored ink. Once the paper has been shredded and made into pulp, air bubbles are injected into it. The ink sticks to the bubbles and rises to the paper's surface, where it can be skimmed off.

Disposable coffee cups have long been banned from recycling centers due a plastic coating that keeps liquid from seeping out of them. In the United Kingdom alone, 2.5 billion of these cups have ended up in landfills each year. Now a British company has developed a process that makes them recyclable. The cup is softened in a warm liquid solution. Then the plastic coating is separated from the paper fiber and skimmed off. The high-grade pulp that remains is remade into quality paper products.

Finding ways to recycle common items such as paper coffee cups can dramatically cut down the amount of trash we produce.

Glass cullet can be made into new bottles or a variety of other products.

GLASS MADE NEW

Crushed glass from beverage bottles and food jars, called cullet, is often unusable for making new bottles and jars because it is **contaminated** with other materials. Some of it ends up as construction material or being used for covering landfills. But today at recycling centers and MRFs, new methods are allowing more glass to be recycled. Magnets pull out metal caps and lids from the stream of glass. Colored glass is then separated out from the more desirable clear glass. Air jets blow the clear glass onto another conveyor belt. The clear crushed glass is sold to bottle manufacturers to be made into new bottles and jars. Thanks to this improved technology, 90 percent of the bottle glass recycled today is used to make new bottles. Companies save millions of dollars by using recycled glass rather than making glass from raw materials.

MODERN MARVEL

Separating recyclables into different containers makes it easier for MRFs to sort and process them.

SINGLE-STREAM RECYCLING

Until about 15 years ago, people had to separate their curbside recyclables into two or more bins. Paper products went in one bin. Plastics, glass, and metal went in another. This is called dual-stream recycling. Recycling trucks had separate compartments into which workers would empty the different bins. But this began to change when single-stream recycling was introduced in the late 1990s. This method allows people to put all their recyclables into a single container. The recyclables are then brought to an MRF to be separated and sorted. Today, many towns and cities have single-stream recycling programs.

HIGH-TECH SEPARATING

At an MRF, new technology helps separate the recyclables so they can be sold to manufacturers and reused. Powerful magnets separate metal products from the single stream. Giant fans blow out paper products. Screens separate flat paper from round containers. Many of these facilities are partially or totally automated, which makes the process move very quickly.

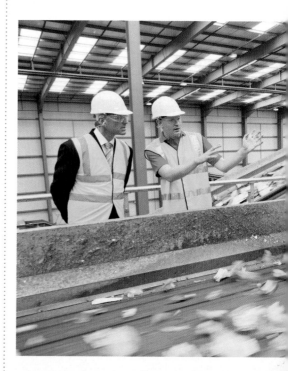

A BETTER WAY

Single-stream recycling encourages more people to participate in recycling. It also makes it easier for workers to collect the recyclables. Finally, single-streaming encourages what experts call "three bin collection." With only one bin needed for recyclables, a second bin can be used for compostable food scraps and yard cuttings. The third bin is for trash. Because so much material goes into the other two bins, much less trash is produced.

In single-stream recycling, all types of recyclables are separated at the recycling facility.

After materials are separated, they are compacted into large bales.

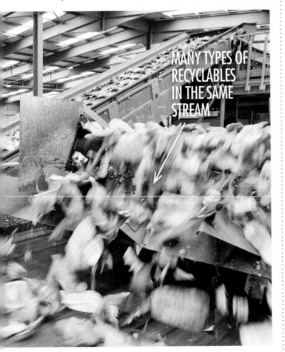

MANY TYPES OF RECYCLABLES IN THE SAME STREAM

THE DOWNSIDE

While single-stream recycling has many advantages, there is still room to improve this process. Cross-contamination of glass, metal, and plastics can occur, which lowers the value of recyclables. Experts estimate that single-stream recycling costs $3.00 more per ton of recyclables than dual-stream recycling. However, as technology improves, this cross-contamination may be largely eliminated.

Every year, millions of plastic bottles end up in landfills instead of recycling centers.

NEW PROCESSES FOR PLASTICS

Plastic is a popular material for making many products because it is so cheap and durable. However, not all plastics are the same. Some are easy to recycle. Others are not. Some are safe to use with food and drinks, while others can cause health problems.

Because there are so many different kinds of plastic recyclables, sorting them is critical. When done by hand, this process can be extremely time-consuming. However, scientists at Ludwig-Maximilian University in Munich, Germany, have found a way to speed things up. A flash of light beamed on each plastic item causes it to **fluoresce**, or glow. Special sensors measure how long it takes for the fluorescence to fade. Each plastic type fluoresces for a different amount of time. This allows the sensors to instantly identify and sort the different types of plastic.

THE PLASTIC BAG PROBLEM

Plastic shopping bags are a major source of waste in the world today. An estimated 100 billion of these flimsy containers are discarded in the United States alone each year. They choke landfills. They suffocate animals in the wild. They are eaten by fish and other sea life, killing them. They are also a tremendous waste of resources. It takes 11 barrels of oil to produce a ton of plastic bags.

Increasing use of easily recyclable paper bags and reusable cloth bags is beginning to solve the problem. Scientists are also developing plastic bags that **biodegrade** much faster than regular plastic bags. Oxo-biodegradable plastic is one of the best of these new inventions. Additives in the plastic cause it to break down when exposed to sunlight or heat. Bacteria and other microscopic creatures can then easily digest the plastic. Disposed bags could degrade completely within a year. The bags are also easy to recycle and make into other plastic products.

Reusable shopping bags help conserve natural resources by cutting down on the amount of plastic that people use.

MODERN MARVEL

SOLAR PANELS

WHEEL SPINS TO POWER CONVEYOR BELT THAT LIFTS TRASH FROM THE WATER

The Inner Harbor Water Wheel prevents trash from reaching the Atlantic Ocean.

A NEW KIND OF WATERWHEEL

The waterwheel is one of the wonders of early human technology. This device uses the power of running water to grind grain and other raw resources in mills. But in Baltimore, Maryland, a new use has been found for this historic machine: keeping trash out of the ocean. The Inner Harbor Water Wheel sits at the mouth of the Jones Falls River, where the river flows into the harbor and then the Atlantic Ocean. Rivers like the Jones Falls carry tons of trash, especially plastic bags, into the sea where they can harm fish and other sea

Trash catches on ridges in the wheel's conveyor belt and is lifted out of the water.

life. The bags and other garbage enter the waterway via storm drains from the ground and streets.

CATCHING THE TRASH

As the river flows, it causes the wheel to turn. When the water current isn't strong enough to turn the wheel, solar cells use the sun's energy to make it spin. Compartments in the wheel trap the trash, lift it out of the water, and deposit it into a barge that serves as a dumpster. When the barge is full, a boat tows it to a waste-to-energy plant. There, the trash is burned to provide electricity for nearby homes and businesses. A new, empty barge immediately replaces the full one. Every day, the Baltimore waterwheel removes as much as 50,000 pounds (22,678 kilograms) of trash from the river, or more than 9,000 tons each year. In the future, similar wheels could be used to help keep other waterways clean. ✳

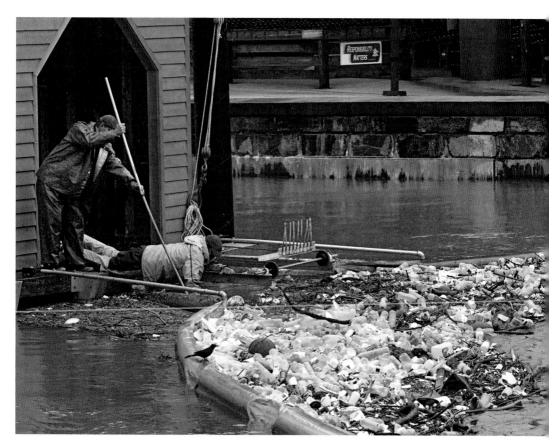

Workers clear out the waterwheel after it became clogged with an excess of trash after a rainstorm in 2008.

METAL MAGIC

After plastics, metal is the biggest waste problem we face today. Aluminum cans are an especially major issue. It takes 500 years for one of these cans to biodegrade in a landfill. The good news is that more and more aluminum is being recycled. Making an aluminum can from recycled metal uses 90 percent less energy than making a new can from raw materials. In addition, aluminum can be recycled over and over again endlessly. However, different cans contain different **alloys**. They must be sorted before being recycled to avoid mixing them together.

Manual sorting is slow and costly. So scientists at the Palo Alto Research Center (PARC) in California have come up with a quicker way to identify alloys and sort metal. They have developed a substance that electrically "excites" each item, quickly identifying its alloys. Current x-ray fluorescence techniques take more than a minute to analyze the alloys in metal objects. The PARC equipment can do it in one-tenth of a second.

Aluminum cans are crushed and compacted into blocks that can be easily transported.

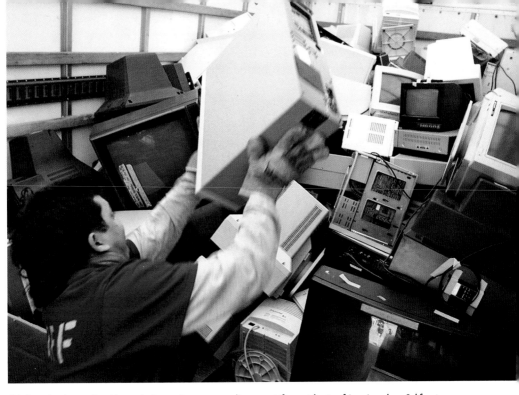

Workers load a truck with used electronics at a recycling event for residents of Los Angeles, California.

E-WASTE

Recycling bottles, cans, and newspapers is one thing. But what should people do with old computers, TV sets, and cell phones? Millions of Americans simply drop these items off at the local dump or landfill. This electronic waste, known as e-waste, is an ongoing challenge, and the problem is growing daily.

One answer is to donate your old electronics to people who could use them. Computers and cell phones often have a lot of life left in them, even after we replace them with newer models. Charities and schools can use them. There are also companies that send used electronic devices overseas to schools and communities in developing countries where they are desperately needed. If you can't donate, you should take your discarded electronics to a recycling center, where they can be either disassembled for recyclables and reusable parts or disposed of responsibly.

Recycling is becoming more and more popular as people realize its many benefits.

CHAPTER THREE

ON THE JOB

As the challenge of conserving resources, protecting the environment, and reducing waste becomes a primary concern for Americans, more people will be needed to work in this important industry. According to government statistics, around 1.1 million people are employed in the collecting, processing, manufacturing, and reusing of recyclable materials today. This number will continue to grow as communities fully commit to recycling. From the drivers who operate recycling trucks to the line workers at MRFs to the engineers and scientists who are working to improve recycling methods, many different workers are needed to keep the recycling stream flowing effectively.

LEGAL MILESTONES

1657	1899	1986	2007
New Amsterdam, which later became New York City, passes a law against residents throwing garbage into the streets.	Dumping garbage in navigable waterways is restricted under the federal Rivers and Harbors Act.	Rhode Island establishes the first statewide mandatory recycling law in the United States.	San Francisco becomes the first American city to ban the distribution of plastic bags in grocery stores.

Scientists collect water samples and test them in the lab to ensure that recycling facilities follow environmental regulations.

SCIENTISTS OF RECYCLING

No matter how effective they are, all waste management programs impact natural and human environments. It is the job of environmental scientists to study and measure that impact, report their findings, and work with government and businesses to lessen it.

Government agencies employ scientists to see that recycling and waste management companies are meeting regulations to protect human health and the environment. Environmental chemists and biologists analyze water and soil samples where waste is given off by recycling processes. They evaluate the impact of chemicals in the environment and design ways to reduce waste and clean up existing pollution. This helps keep the environment safe for plant, animal, and human life.

Other scientists study materials to find new ways of recycling them. This might mean creating new types of plastic that are more easily recycled, finding new ways to break materials down so they can be reused, and much more.

REUSING RARE EARTH METALS

Many products are made using valuable materials that are difficult to remove and reuse. For example, rare earth metals, used in computers, televisions, and other electronic products, are in short supply in many parts of the world. These materials are built into the products and intertwined with many other substances in a complex arrangement. Recycling them isn't as simple as putting them on a conveyor belt and letting a machine sort them. Scientists are always searching for new ways to harvest these materials so they don't go to waste. At a Belgian university, environmental chemists have developed a process for extracting two kinds of rare earth metals from fluorescent lamps. By using a special chemical **solvent**, they have been able to successfully extract the rare earth metals from the lamps, remove poisonous mercury from them, and reuse them in color television screens and lamps.

Circuit boards for electronic devices contain valuable rare earth metals that should be recycled.

ENGINEERS OF ALL KINDS

Mechanical and electrical engineers design recycling machines and equipment. They constantly find ways to improve these machines to make them more effective by consuming less energy and fewer raw materials.

One thing they are currently focusing on is finding more ways to automate the recycling process. With fewer workers sorting and dealing with recyclables, the process is faster and safer.

Civil engineers help design buildings that make the best use of resources and energy. Environmental engineers work on new ways to manage and reduce industrial waste produced by MRFs or manufacturers that use recycled materials. They also investigate companies that are accused of violating environmental regulations. They work with the company and government officials to achieve a positive outcome. If actions are needed to correct the problem, the engineers assist or oversee these efforts.

Many new buildings are constructed using recycled materials, such as the metal roof on this building.

Foam products may be convenient and cheap, but they clog our landfills.

PRODUCT DESIGNERS

New recyclable products and products made from recycled materials are constantly arriving in stores. Product designers are in charge of creating and testing these products. They also come up with new ways to recycle, sometimes finding ways to recycle products that have in the past been unrecyclable.

For many years, Styrofoam was not recyclable. Yet this light plastic substance is used worldwide to make plates, coffee cups, packing material, and other products. Styrofoam is not biodegradable. It also contains a chemical called benzene that can cause cancer. However, product designers have recently found a way to shred Styrofoam safely and melt it down under high heat. Then it can be remolded safely into other products. This could help cut down on the amount of Styrofoam that ends up in landfills.

Sherill Baldwin is an environmental analyst with Connecticut's Department of Energy and Environmental Protection. She works on construction and demolition debris recycling, product stewardship, and reuse projects. She has 30 years of experience working in waste management.

When did you first realize you wanted to work in the recycling industry? I grew up in Harwich, Massachusetts, on Cape Cod, where my mother was a naturalist. When I was a child, my mother would walk the wetlands with my brothers and me, and we'd pick up buried objects, tiny treasures such as broken dishes and old medicine bottles. I didn't realize it at the time, but the wetlands my mother was working to preserve were on the site of an old dump. That was my introduction to how we throw away stuff that is valuable.

What did you study in college to prepare you for a career in the recycling industry? I wanted to learn more about waste management and recycling after living in California for a couple of years after high school. I came back to Massachusetts and entered UMass at Amherst in 1989. At the time, they had no major in solid waste management and recycling wasn't widely seen as a career. I had to create my own degree, putting together classes in engineering, business, planning, environmental science, organic agriculture, and policy.

What did you learn in other jobs you held in school that helped you in your career? I went to UMass because I heard they had a recycling club. I soon found out that it had been inactive for five years! So I started up the club again. Soon the university hired me to develop a recycling program for student dormitories and off-campus housing. After graduation, I went to work for the Center for EcoTechnology in Pittsfield, Massachusetts, where the focus was on composting or organics recycling. Then I entered the University of Michigan to earn a degree in resource development. I came back to New England and had several interesting jobs. For a while, I was the ecology director at a spiritual retreat center in Madison, Connecticut. I've been working for the state of Connecticut for seven years.

What project have you worked on that you're especially proud of? The deconstruction industry. It involves dismantling homes and reusing the building materials instead of demolishing them and tossing them into a landfill. The materials that are recovered are sold at building material reuse centers so homeowners and contractors can purchase the used doors, windows, appliances, and flooring for reuse. We have nine reuse centers in Connecticut and hope to see more of them in the future.

It takes a team of people to produce a good recycling program. Does working as part of a team come naturally to you, and how do you handle the other team members when you're the boss? I love collaboration. You learn a lot more that way. When diverse people come together, they have different ideas. Dialogues help get them to the nugget, the concept where all can agree. From there, the group can move forward.

What would your dream project be if you were given unlimited resources? I volunteer for a creative reuse center for the arts, which sells low-cost art supplies to teachers, artists, and the public. The materials are scrap and surplus from industry and businesses. If I could, I would work more with folks who make art or interesting products from scrap.

What advice would you give to young people who want to work in the field of recycling? I would tell them to study a range of subjects in school, because waste management involves everything. Garbage is very personal. You are, in a real sense, what you throw away. When you look into your trash can, you learn a lot about yourself. ☀

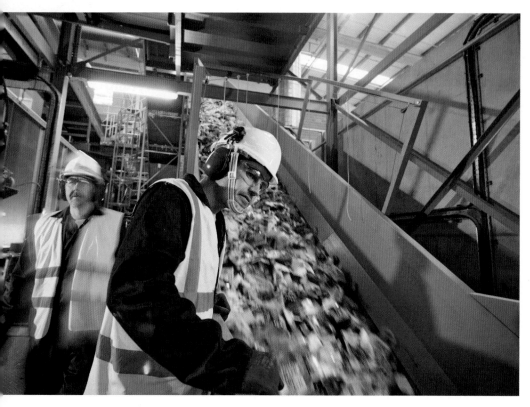

MRF employees keep watch over automated sorting machines to make sure they are functioning correctly.

PICKING UP AND PICKING OUT

Many skilled workers are needed to get recyclables to MRFs and process them. Drivers operate recycling trucks as other workers empty the recycling bins into the vehicle. Route managers plot out the truck routes, plan schedules for pickup, and record statistics and data.

At the MRF, sorters separate the different recyclables onto conveyor belts. If the facility is automated, workers are still needed to keep an eye on things and pull out any items that could damage the machinery. Mechanics, technicians, and maintenance workers inspect, repair, and maintain all equipment, including the recycling trucks. Mechanics may be called on to make emergency roadside repairs if a truck breaks down along its route.

MANAGING AND SELLING

MRF managers ensure that facilities run smoothly and that the flow of recyclables is efficient and profitable. They develop budgets, set long-term goals, and deal with the public and the press. They also are responsible for recruiting, hiring, and training workers. Managers evaluate workers' performance and share their feedback with senior managers. They make sure the workplace is safe and give regular safety briefings to workers.

Some companies specialize in purchasing recyclables so they can process them and sell the recycled materials. Sales representatives, also called account managers, find landfills and other facilities that will sell recyclables. After the recyclables are processed into raw materials, the sales representatives seek out businesses and manufacturers who want to buy them. These representatives need to be persuasive salespeople who can give a convincing presentation to potential clients.

A manager supervises other employees and makes sure the recycling operation is working smoothly.

THE ARTISTIC SIDE

Erika Iris Simmons reuses old cassette tapes to create portraits of stars such as rock musician Jimi Hendrix.

Reusing old things can be a dirty business. However, some people have found ways to create beautiful things using materials that might seem like nothing more than old junk. For example, many of today's artists and craftspeople are finding creative ways to take e-waste of the 1980s and 1990s and upcycle it into works of art and useful products.

UPSCALING THE PAST

Chicago artist Erika Iris Simmons has found a new use for old audiotapes and videocassettes. She spools out the tape and uses it to create portraits of famous people.

Los Angeles designer Chris McCullough also uses old tapes in his art projects. He makes celebrity portraits out of audiocassette cases arranged like tiles. McCullough says he finds it appropriate because "cassettes represent the first portable music medium you could share and personalize yourself."

Ptolemy Elrington hopes his sculptures will encourage people to think about their own personal impact on the environment.

FLOOR LAMPS AND AQUARIUMS

Other artists use large pieces of e-waste to create useful items. Jeff Faber of Oshkosh, Wisconsin, turns old video game consoles such as the Nintendo 64 into lamps. Jake Harris of Hildreth, Nebraska, transforms old computers into aquariums. Other artists convert computer towers into mailboxes and outdoor benches, or computer circuit boards into wall and desk clocks.

Yuken Teruya poses with a tree he sculpted from paper shopping bags.

JUNKYARD SCULPTURES

Some artists transform trash into works of fine art. Michelle Reader of London, England, upcycles materials such as the internal parts of mechanical toys and clocks into sculptures. "I love the unpredictability of found materials and enjoy the invention necessary to transfer them into a sculpture," she says.

Ptolemy Elrington's favorite medium is old car hubcaps. He bends, shapes, and fuses them together to make a shiny fish or a fierce wild boar with pointy tusks.

Yuken Teruya prefers to work with paper products. His *Corner Forest* is composed of tree branches cut from toilet paper rolls and mounted on a wall. His *Constellation* is made up of dark skies of stars fashioned inside paper shopping bags. ✷

SPECIALISTS AND RESEARCHERS

Many people need to be convinced to recycle. They might not be aware of how important and easy it is. Recycling specialists are the public face of recycling. They are employed by environmental service organizations or government agencies. They attend events where recycling and preserving the environment are the focus. They speak to community groups, schools, homeowners' associations, and other organizations to emphasize the importance of recycling programs. They also help prepare educational materials for distribution.

Recycling researchers conduct research on recycled products. They collect data on market demand for products as well as the time and cost required to recycle different items. This information helps them develop plans to improve the recycling facilities that employ them.

Recycling specialists might hold meetings to discuss the best ways of informing people about recycling programs.

Drivers need to get special licenses before they are allowed to operate large vehicles such as recycling trucks.

EDUCATION AND TRAINING

The education requirements for jobs in the recycling and reuse industry vary widely. Scientists and engineers need at least a bachelor's degree. Many of them also have more advanced degrees, and they must continually learn new things throughout their careers to stay in touch with the field's latest developments.

Mechanics and technicians should have at least a high school diploma and a year of on-the-job experience repairing and operating machinery. MRF managers need a bachelor's degree. Many also have a master's degree in business administration or industrial engineering.

Route managers may be hired with a high school education, but would benefit by having several years of experience in waste management or transportation. Drivers need to be high school graduates and should have a commercial driver's license. No specific educational requirements are generally needed for haulers and sorters. However, these workers need to be strong enough to lift heavy bins and items off a conveyor belt.

Recyclables have a long journey to become new products after they are tossed in bins.

WE RECYCLE

WE RECYCLE

CHAPTER FOUR

FROM CURBSIDE TO STORE SHELF

The journey of a recyclable from the consumer who first uses it to the store shelf as a new product is long and eventful. Three important things must happen in any recycling process. The recyclables must first be collected. Then they are treated and processed, sold to manufacturers, and made into new products. Finally, they are put back in circulation. Let's follow the path from your home to the store and see just how recycling works.

HIGHLIGHTS IN RECYCLING TECHNOLOGY

1894	1905	Early 1970s	Late 1990s
One of the first returnable deposit glass bottles is manufactured by the Biedenharn Candy Company of Vicksburg, Mississippi.	New York City burns garbage to generate enough electricity to light the Williamsburg Bridge.	The first recycling trailers pulled behind a garbage truck appear in American towns and cities.	The first single-stream recycling facilities begin operating.

COLLECTING AND DEPOSITING

It's Friday morning, time to put the garbage out for pickup. Along with your trash can, you also carry a bin of recyclables down to the curb. In your neighborhood, recyclables are collected every other week. Your transfer station accepts single streaming, so your bin contains paper, plastic, metal, and glass.

As you set down the bin, you notice the bottle of fruit juice for which you paid an added nickel deposit. You'd like to get that nickel back. So you remove it from the bin and take it down to your local supermarket, along with some other deposit bottles and cans you had set aside earlier. The market has its own recycling center with machines that accept glass and plastic bottles and aluminum cans. You slip a bottle into the slot in the machine and hear it drop and break inside. When you've finished recycling all your bottles, you press a button and the machine gives you a receipt for the total amount of your deposits. You can spend the amount on the receipt as credit in the market.

Taking your recycling bins to the curb or your local recycling center is just the first step in the recycling process.

Trucks unload materials into piles at a recycling center in New York City.

TO THE TRANSFER STATION

The shredded plastic, broken glass, and crushed cans from the store recycling machines will be removed once the machine is full. These materials are then collected and delivered to a manufacturer to be made into new products.

The bins the recycling truck picks up at your curbside have a longer journey. They are first brought to your town's transfer station and unloaded from the trucks into large dumpsters. Once they are full, the dumpsters are loaded onto flatbed trucks and delivered to an MRF. There the recyclables will be sorted and bundled.

WHERE THE MAGIC HAPPENS

A Recology employee sorts materials at an MRF in San Francisco.

RECOLOGY

Among the U.S. cities most committed to recycling is San Francisco, California. San Francisco's success in reducing waste is due in large part to Recology. This waste mangagement company, owned and operated by its employees, is on the cutting edge of recycling. With Recology's help, San Francisco has reduced its discarded waste from 900,000 tons in 2000 to nearly half that by 2009. By 2020, the city hopes to become America's first zero-waste community.

THREE BINS

Recology has given every city household three bins to fill. The blue bin is for all accepted recyclable products. The green

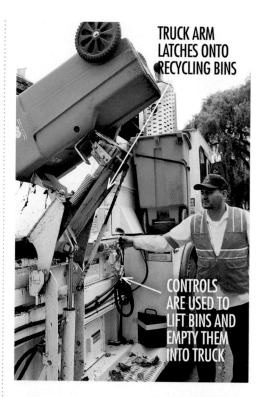

TRUCK ARM LATCHES ONTO RECYCLING BINS

CONTROLS ARE USED TO LIFT BINS AND EMPTY THEM INTO TRUCK

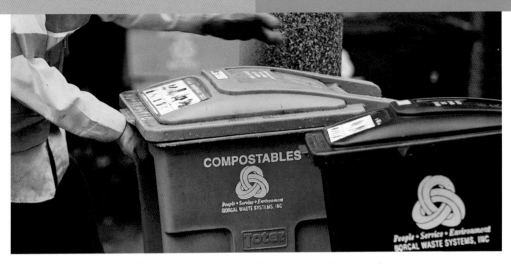

Color-coded bins make it easy for people to separate recyclables, compostables, and trash.

bin is for food scraps, plant material, and paper that has been soiled by food. The black bin is for trash that doesn't fit into those categories.

People in San Francisco are required to participate in this program. Those who don't put out their bins or separate recyclables properly are given a warning, If they still don't follow the rules after receiving a warning, a fine is imposed. To educate the public on this program, Recology sends representatives to meet with residents and provides a lively online video that explains recycling.

ADVISE AND CONSULT

Recology sells its compost materials to area farms and vineyards to be used as fertilizer for soil. For a fee, reps will advise farmers on how to best use the compost to benefit crops. Recology is considering creating a consulting division to handle the many inquiries from visiting officials who want to learn how to bring better recycling methods to their own cities and countries. The company's goal is to retire every landfill in California and eventually the entire nation. "To me, that's not waste management," Recology president and CEO Michael J. Sangiacomo says of landfills. "It's just putting waste in a hole in the ground and hoping nothing goes wrong. If you can put waste back into commerce, that's much smarter.

Composting produces a rich, soil-like material that helps plants grow.

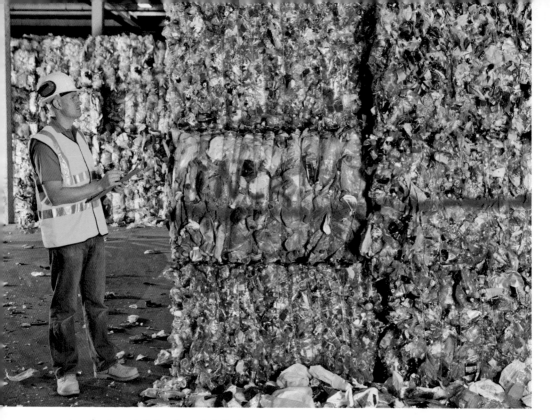
A worker inspects bales of recycled plastic.

ON TO THE MRF

At the MRF, recyclables travel along conveyor belts where the sorting begins. First, cardboard boxes and plastic bags are removed from the stream so they won't jam the automated sorting machines. Heavier metals and glass products are separated from lighter plastics and paper. The paper stream is separated into newspapers, glossy magazine paper, computer paper, and scrap paper. Magnets are used to separate metals containing iron, such as tin and steel cans, from those that do not contain iron, such as aluminum cans. The magnets attract the iron objects and repel the non-iron ones. Both will be recycled. Glass is separated by color—clear, amber, green, and brown. Once sorted, each kind of recyclable is ready to be bundled or baled. Then it is sold and shipped to manufacturers that will break the recyclables down into their raw materials to make new products.

FROM PAPER TO PULP

Papermaking companies shred recycled paper and place it in machines called pulpers along with water and chemicals. The liquid is heated to quickly break down the paper into fibers. The result is a soupy pulp. The pulp is forced through screens that remove such contaminants as glue and plastic. Next it enters rapidly spinning cone-shaped cylinders. Heavy contaminants such as staples and paper clips fly out of the cone, while smaller ones are collected in the center and later removed. Water is used to rinse any remaining ink from the pulp.

The pulp is beaten to further break down the fibers into smaller pieces. Any dye is then stripped from color paper using chemicals. This turns the pulp brown. If white paper is desired, the pulp is bleached using more chemicals. This pulp can be used to make new paper.

A worker shows off paper pulp at a factory in the Netherlands.

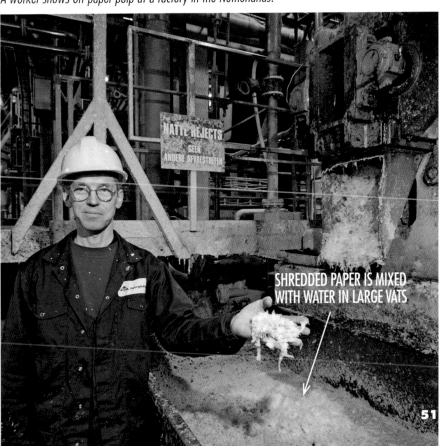

SHREDDED PAPER IS MIXED WITH WATER IN LARGE VATS

LASTING CONTRIBUTION

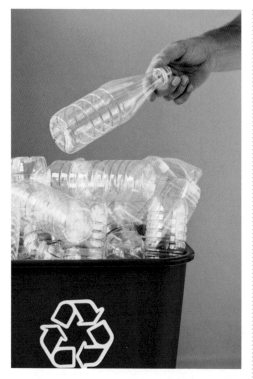

You have probably used one of Craig Busch's classic blue recycling bins.

THE BLUE BIN

Recycling technology has advanced in many ways since the early 1980s. However, one thing has not changed—the bright blue recycling bins left curbside in towns and cities across North America. The blue bin was the invention of Craig Busch, a Canadian college student. Curbside pickup was a new program in Canada at the time. Busch came up with a lightweight, durable bin that people could fill with recyclables. In 1981, the blue bins were used for the first time in test neighborhoods in Kitchener, Ontario.

A CURBSIDE EXPERIMENT

The Kitchener government experimented with several different methods of curbside pickup. In one, the blue bins were used. In another, no blue bins were provided. The blue bin proved the most popular option among the townspeople. Two years later,

Recycling containers of all kinds are colored blue today because of Craig Busch's original design.

Blue recycling bins usually display the universal recycling logo.

the entire town was provided with blue bins. In 1985, Busch and a partner started Busch Systems to manufacture recycling bins on a large scale. Soon the blue bins were appearing across Canada and the United States.

WHY BLUE?

Busch picked the color blue not only because it looked nice but also because it would be easy for truck drivers to see. Blue also proved best in withstanding damage and fading from exposure to the Sun's **ultraviolet** light as bins sat at the curb. Originally the blue bins were manufactured in only one size. Because recycling has grown more popular, they are now available in many different sizes to accommodate people's different needs. Many state and local governments provide residents with one free bin, with the option to purchase more if needed. Along with the blue color, the bins still display the universal recycling logo and the proud words "WE RECYCLE." ✳

GLASS AND METAL MADE ANEW

At a glassmaking plant, crushed glass is ground down into cullet. All contaminants must be removed from the cullet before it can be processed. A magnetic field removes metal bottle caps. Any bits of plastic or paper are removed by hand or machine. Fine screens filter out any ceramic bits. At this point, the cleaned cullet is melted down and decolorized with chemicals. If a new color is needed, the cullet is dyed. The cullet is sold to manufacturers who melt it and place it into molds, letting it harden into new jars, bottles, and other objects. When these are discarded, the recycling process is repeated. Glass can be recycled forever. This is a very good feature, since glass bottles will never decompose in a landfill.

At a processing plant, aluminum cans are melted down. Then the molten aluminum is hardened into giant blocks called ingots. Each ingot is composed of about 1.6 million beverage cans. The ingots go to mills. There, they are rolled out into thin layers and used to make new products. Aluminum can be recycled faster than any other material. The entire process can take less than 60 days.

A worker inspects aluminum ingots at a warehouse.

Plastic pellets can be molded into new plastic products.

PLASTICS TRANSFORMED

Plastic bottles and containers are put through a machine where sharp blades chip or shred them into tiny pieces. Plastic bags are also cut apart. However, they are chopped up using large blades. The bits of plastic are washed in a strong solution of water and detergents to remove all liquid residue and paper labels. The pieces are then melted down and put through a machine called an extruder. The extruder molds the melted plastic into thin tubes that resemble noodles. Spinning knives cut the tubes into small pellets. The pellets can be molded into new plastic products. Some become bottles again. Others become such diverse products as kitchenware, countertops, and outdoor furniture.

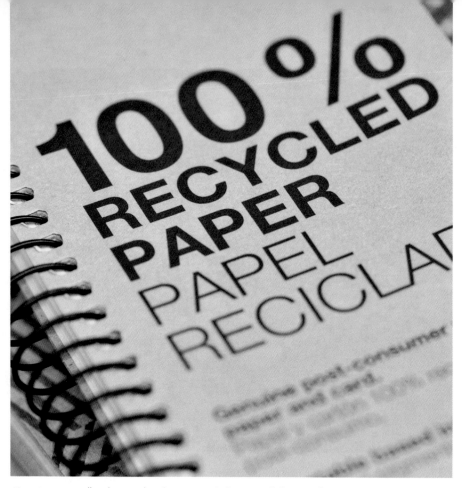

Many items proudly advertise that they are made from recycled materials.

BACK ON THE SHELF

Once the products are finished, they are sold and shipped out to stores across the country. Manufacturers mark recycled products, especially paper and plastic items, with symbols and codes that inform shoppers they are made from recyclables. Look for these items at stores. When you buy a recycled product, you are helping the environment and giving your support to the recycling industry. You are also sending a message to manufacturers that they should create more goods using recycled materials. The next time you buy a bottle of fruit juice, think about the recycled glass that made it. And don't forget to return it for your deposit!

SUMMING UP

Recycling is off to a good start. But we still have a long way to go. Too many people continue to toss bottles, cans, and other recyclables into their garbage cans, and these items end up clogging landfills. Other trash ends up in waterways, polluting them and killing fish and plants. Garbage burned in incinerators sends toxins into the air we breathe. Garbage pollutes our entire environment.

In addition, precious energy and resources are expended making new products instead of reusing or recycling old ones. While recycling should be a global effort, it has to start with individuals. How can you do a better job of reusing the resources in your life? Or even better, maybe you'd like to help out by getting a job in the recycling industry one day. If each of us pitches in and recycles, a society with zero waste may become a reality.

Pollution, a major problem everywhere, could be substantially reduced by a worldwide commitment to recycling.

THE FUTURE

Plasma arc recycling uses high heat to turn discarded products into energy.

PLASMA ARC RECYCLING

While turning recyclable products into new products is important, scientists have discovered that many discarded products, including nonrecyclable ones, can be turned into energy. Plasma arc recycling heats solid waste at extremely high temperatures. This produces a gas that can be burned for energy as well as a hard, rocklike substance that can be made into a building material. Because the temperatures are so high, most of the toxic chemicals in the products are burned away.

Plasma arc recycling is fairly rare today. The process is still controversial. Some critics claim that despite precautions, it still releases harmful chemicals into the atmosphere. The most successful plasma arc recycling plant opened in England in 2007.

A WATER-RECYCLING SHOWER

New inventions are improving recycling. One of the most interesting is a water-recycling shower created by several inventors in Britain and Sweden over the past several years. Daily showering is one of the greatest wastes of fresh water in many countries. This innovative shower cleans, filters, and recycles 70 percent of the water it uses. In an average four-person household, it could save 20,000 to 40,000 gallons (75,708 to 151,416 liters) of water every year.

RECYCLING APPS

Encouraging more people to recycle is a top priority. Participants in the 2014 Recycling Challenge came up with some original Web apps that could motivate people to recycle. One proposed app, called CycleUp, would give each resident of a community a ranking based on how much he or she recycles. It would rate everybody against their neighbors, to spark friendly competition. The app would also encourage entire neighborhoods to compete against one another within their city for first place in recycling. Another app would tell users how to recycle a product when they scan its bar code into their phone. They would also receive information about why this product should be recycled.

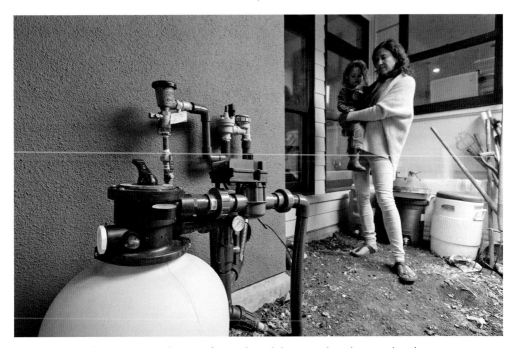

Some water recycling systems use the water from sinks and showers to keep lawns and gardens green.

CAREER STATS

ENVIRONMENTAL SCIENTISTS

MEDIAN ANNUAL SALARY (2012): $63,570

NUMBER OF JOBS (2012): 90,000

PROJECTED JOB GROWTH (2012–2022): 15%, faster than average

PROJECTED INCREASE IN JOBS (2012–2022): 13,200

REQUIRED EDUCATION: Bachelor's degree

LICENSE/CERTIFICATION: None

ENVIRONMENTAL ENGINEERING TECHNICIANS

MEDIAN ANNUAL SALARY (2012): $43,350

NUMBER OF JOBS (2012): 19,000

PROJECTED JOB GROWTH (2012–2022): 18%, faster than average

PROJECTED INCREASE IN JOBS (2012–2022): 3,500

REQUIRED EDUCATION: Associate's degree

LICENSE/CERTIFICATION: None

MRF HANDLERS AND SORTERS

MEDIAN ANNUAL SALARY (2012): $22,970

NUMBER OF JOBS (2012): 3,428,800

PROJECTED JOB GROWTH (2012–2022): 10%, as fast as average

PROJECTED INCREASE IN JOBS (2012–2022): 341,700

REQUIRED EDUCATION: Less than high school

LICENSE/CERTIFICATION: None

Figures reported by the United States Bureau of Labor Statistics

RESOURCES

BOOKS

Green, Robert. *From Waste to Energy*. Ann Arbor, MI: Cherry Lake Publishing, 2013.

Mooney, Carla. *Recycling*. Chicago: Norwood House Press, 2014.

Palmer, Erin. *Recycling, Yes or No*. Vero Beach, FL: Rourke Educational Media, 2015.

FACTS FOR NOW

Visit this Scholastic Web site for more information on recycling and upcycling:
www.factsfornow.scholastic.com
Enter the keywords **Recycling and Upcycling**

GLOSSARY

alloys (AL-oiz) metals made from mixing other metals, or mixing a metal with an element that is not a metal

biodegrade (bye-oh-di-GRAYD) break down by natural processes

compost (KAHM-post) a mixture of organic material, such as rotted leaves, vegetables, or manure, that is added to soil to make it more productive

conservation (kahn-sur-VAY-shuhn) the protection of valuable things, especially forests, wildlife, natural resources, or artistic or historic objects

contaminated (kuhn-TAM-i-nay-tid) containing harmful or undesirable substances

dumps (DUHMPS) areas of land where people deposit garbage without any environmental protection, compaction, or plan for completion

epidemics (ep-i-DEM-iks) infectious diseases present in a large number of people at the same time

fluoresce (fluh-RESS) to release radiation in the form of visible light

municipal (myoo-NISS-uh-puhl) relating to a town or city or its local government

pulp (PUHLP) any soft, wet mixture

rationed (RASH-uhnd) gave out resources in limited amounts

sanitation (san-i-TAY-shuhn) systems for cleaning the water supply and disposing of sewage and garbage in a town or city

solvent (SAHL-vuhnt) a substance, usually a liquid, that can make another substance dissolve

transfer station (TRANS-fur STAY-shuhn) a holding area from which trash is taken to a landfill or a Materials Recovery Facility

ultraviolet (uhl-truh-VYE-uh-lit) a type of light that cannot be seen by the human eye

upcycle (UHP-sye-kuhl) to put a discarded product to a new use

INDEX

Page numbers in *italics* indicate illustrations.

INDEX (CONTINUED)

ABOUT THE AUTHOR

STEVEN OTFINOSKI has written more than 175 books for young readers, including books on forensics, computers, and rockets. He fills his recycling bins every week and uses cloth bags at the supermarket. He lives in Connecticut.

We're always happy to hear from you. For questions or comments concerning the editorial content of this book, please write to:

Rodale Book Readers' Service
33 East Minor Street
Emmaus, PA 18098

Look for other Rodale books wherever books are sold. Or call us at (800) 848-4735.

For more information about Rodale Organic Gardening magazine and books, visit us at:

www.organicgardening.com

Editor: Karen Costello Soltys
Contributing Editor: Christine Bucks
Interior Book Designer: Nancy Smola Blitcliff
Cover Designer: Patricia Field
Photography Editor: Lyn Horst
Layout Designer: Dale Mack
Researchers: Sarah Wolfgang Heffner,
    Pamela Ruch, and Heidi A. Stonehill
Copy Editors: Sarah Dunn and Stacey Follin
Manufacturing Coordinator: Mark Krahforst
Indexer: Nan Badgett
Editorial Assistance: Kerrie A. Cadden

RODALE ORGANIC GARDENING BOOKS
Managing Editor: Fern Marshall Bradley
Executive Creative Director: Christin Gangi
Art Director: Patricia Field
Production Manager: Robert V. Anderson Jr.
Studio Manager: Leslie M. Keefe
Associate Copy Manager: Jennifer Hornsby
Manufacturing Manager: Mark Krahforst

**Library of Congress
    Cataloging-in-Publication Data**
    Rodale organic gardening basics. Roses /
from the editors of Rodale Organic Gardening
Magazine and Books.
        p.   cm.
    Includes bibliographical references (p.   )
and index.
    ISBN 0-87596-839-2 (pbk. : alk. paper)
    1. Rose culture. 2. Organic gardening.
I. Rodale Books.
SB411 .O75 2000
635.9'33734—dc21   99—050445

Distributed in the book trade by St. Martin's Press

2 4 6 8 10 9 7 5 3 1 paperback

roses

RODALE

**From the Editors of
Rodale Organic Gardening
Magazine and Books**

contents

True Confessions of an Organic Rose Grower

More than any other plant, roses are what people think they can't grow organically. Tell that to my garden in June when the rosebushes are bursting with the most fragrant beauty you can imagine. Or in September when the last roses of the season grace my garden with their romance.

Success in growing roses requires three things: picking the right roses, giving them the right environment, and having no fear. After all, a rosebush costs less than a dozen cut roses (which you *know* are going to die).

The right environment for roses involves manure (roses love it), garlic (insect pests hate it), and lots of sun. So plant your roses where they'll get plenty of sun, put a pile of composted manure around your roses every spring or fall, plant garlic cloves around the base of the bushes, and read this book for even more tips and techniques to make growing and enjoying roses easy and rewarding.

One of my favorite roses comes from my mother-in-law's garden. It survived more than 40 winters growing near Rochester, New York. Now it's growing in my Pennsylvania garden. No one knows what it's called or where it came from originally. But whenever I smell its powerful fragrance, I think of her, and I hope that 40 years from now, my daughters will be enjoying it in their gardens, too.

Happy organic gardening!

Maria Rodale

> **Success in growing roses requires three things: picking the right roses, giving them the right environment, and having no fear.**

You can enjoy the elegant beauty and sumptuous fragrance of roses in your organic garden as long as you select roses that fit your climate and aren't highly prone to pest and disease problems.

chapter one

Go Organic: Roses Simplified

Welcome to the world of organic rose growing! Growing roses doesn't have to be complicated or scary, as you may been led to believe. Once you learn how to choose the right roses and use organic techniques, you'll find that growing roses is a pleasurable—and beautiful—pastime.

A HEALTHY APPROACH TO GROWING ROSES

Growing roses organically is good for the soil, the roses, and you. After all, you don't need synthetic chemicals to grow beautiful, lush plants with gorgeous blossoms. You simply need rich soil, the right kind of rose for your site, a preventive approach to potential problems, and safe, organic controls for when pests or diseases attack your roses. In this book, you'll find exactly what you need to know about choosing and growing roses the organic way.

6 THINGS YOU CAN STOP DOING NOW

Once you've decided to grow roses organically, you'll discover that it's actually *easier* than growing them conventionally. So read on to learn about the things you can stop (or never start) doing to your roses when you become an organic rose grower.

1. STOP Using Chemicals!

You may have heard that roses need lots of fertilizer, or that it's impossible to grow beautiful roses without continually spraying them with insecticides

Once you've decided to grow roses organically, you'll discover that it's actually *easier* than growing them conventionally.

Your roses can look just as beautiful as these 'Wenlock' (left), 'Queen Nefertiti' (center), and 'Trolius' (right) roses do—without the use of chemical fertilizers or harmful pesticides.

and fungicides. But there are plenty of great *organic* fertilizers for roses, and if you choose roses carefully, they won't need constant spraying to prevent pest and disease problems. So instead of spraying chemicals, build your soil with lots of compost, encourage beneficial, pest-eating insects to visit your garden, and most important, grow disease-resistant roses.

2. STOP Buying on Impulse!

Nothing hooks a gardener better than a blooming rose. But even if you spot a rose at the garden center that's drop-dead gorgeous or that has a wonderful fragrance, resist the impulse to buy. And no matter how tempting those pictures in the catalog may appear, you have no way of knowing what conditions those roses were grown under, or how frequently they were sprayed with chemicals.

There's an amazingly wide variety of roses, and if you don't know what you're buying, you may end up with a rose that won't do well in your yard. For one thing, not all roses are suited for every climate. Some roses are much more susceptible to disease than others. Also, some roses are better suited than others for different uses in the landscape, such as hedges, groundcovers, or shrub borders.

The smart approach to shopping for roses is to decide where and how you want to use roses *before* you buy—and choose from varieties that will do best in your climate. If you spot a cultivar you like, do some research on its resistance to disease so you won't be inviting problems into your garden when you plant it. If you discover that it isn't a great choice, you can always find another rose that blooms in a similar color that is disease-resistant.

'The Fairy' is just one of many low-maintenance roses on the market. It's a low-growing polyantha rose, which is particularly well known for disease resistance.

3. STOP Overwatering!

Watering wisely is key in today's era of water conservation, and that goes for watering roses, too. Even though roses do require a fair amount of water, you can help your roses thrive with less water by applying mulch around the base of the plants and choosing your planting site carefully.

For instance, don't plant roses in spots that you know are very dry or very windy. And if you live in an area with sandy soil or dry summers, improve your soil's water-holding capacity with compost, and choose drought-resistant roses (see "Choosing & Using Roses" on page 7 for more details).

Take the time to mulch around your roses and you'll end up saving watering time. You'll save on your water bill, too.

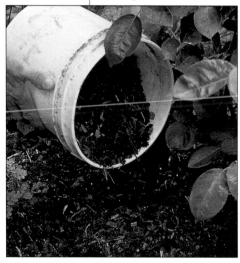

IF YOU GROW a bed that's made up entirely of roses, you might get bored looking at the same thing day after day. Instead, try planting them with other shrubs behind them or with perennials or ground-cover around them. That way you can mix plants with bold and fine foliage to contrast the medium-textured foliage of your roses. A bed with a mix of textures that are glossy and dull, papery and leathery, and smooth and ribbed will hold your eye—and your interest—a lot longer than ones with a single texture. For ideas of what to plant with roses, visit a public rose garden, or look at photographs in books, catalogs, and magazines.

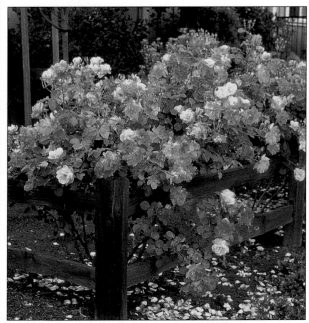

Try planting roses like these 'Joseph's Coat' roses along an entranceway fence, where they'll provide season-long beauty that you, your visitors, and your neighbors all can enjoy.

4. STOP Planting Roses in a Row!

Don't grow your roses in a row as you would tomatoes or peppers. They'll look leggy and unattractive and be more prone to pests and diseases. The introduction of more care-free roses has made it easier than ever for us to rethink their role in the landscape. Instead of relegating the bare-legged hybrid teas to their own corner of the garden, incorporate different varieties of the versatile rose into your landscape by growing them over a fence or arbor, using them as a hedge, or mixing them in with perennials in a flower bed. For more ideas on using roses as attractive landscape plants, see "Landscaping with Roses" on page 71.

5. STOP Inviting Beetles In!

Japanese beetle traps attract not only Japanese beetles but also every other beetle in the neighborhood. So don't set up traps near your rosebushes (the traps aren't very attractive anyway).

If you really want to use these traps, place them at least 50 feet downwind from your plants. That way, you may succeed in your goal of luring the beetles *away* from your roses.

6. STOP Visiting Rose Gardens Only in June!

If you love roses, you've probably taken a trip or two to visit a public rose garden. The most popular time to do this is in June, when all the roses are lush and beautiful, and the scent is downright heady. But before you buy one of each variety you see in its full splendor in June, take a trip back to the rose garden in July and September so you can see which of the roses you like are really garden-worthy—in bloom and out!

Formal rose gardens are beautiful in June, but later in the season, you can see which roses are attractive year-round.

For the best effect, match the rose to the site. 'Alexander Girault' is a climbing rose that graces this entryway trellis, beckoning anyone who passes by to enter the garden within.

chapter two

Choosing & Using Roses

With more than 30,000 rose species and cultivars available, choosing the perfect rose isn't easy! The key is answering the question, "What do I want roses to do for my landscape?" Perhaps you want to dress up a split-rail fence, enhance a perennial garden, or add a colorful accent to a shrub border. There's a rose for almost every landscape purpose, and this chapter will help you decide which varieties are best suited for the project you have in mind.

ALL ROSES AREN'T ALIKE

Before you leap into choosing roses, it's a good idea to learn about the different classes available—what they look like and how they grow and behave. Some roses are small shrubs, while others can grow taller than you. Still other types are long and vining, while some form low groundcovers. The three major categories of roses are species roses, old roses, and modern roses. Read on to learn about these roses and how they might work in your landscape.

Using Species Roses

Species roses are tough and disease-resistant—excellent for a natural area in your yard or a shrub border. They provide a wide variety of choices of size, form, and hardiness. They bloom once, usually in early summer, and form seed-bearing rose hips in the fall.

Species roses are the original roses. About 200 different species roses exist. In general, species roses bear single, five-petaled flowers, and they self-pollinate. (So if you plant seeds from species roses, the offspring should be identical to the parent plant.)

> **Some roses are small shrubs, while others can grow taller than you. Still other types are long and vining, while some form low ground-covers.**

7

Rosa macrantha is a once-blooming species rose that bears pale pink, single blooms followed by quite showy hips. Its flexible canes make it a great choice to train as a groundcover.

'Mme. Isaac Pereire', a very fragrant bourbon rose, is an excellent choice to train to a pillar or other tall structure. It blooms in early summer and again in fall.

Using Old Roses

Old roses are usually very fragrant, have a pleasing plant shape, and are tough, long-lasting shrubs. Common types of old roses include alba, Bourbon, damask, China, and gallica.

The drawback to planting old roses is that many bloom only once a year, usually in early summer. Although they look and smell beautiful, their blooms don't last long.

Using Modern Roses

Unlike species roses and some old roses, modern roses bloom all summer, so you get nonstop color and landscape impact. But summer-long beauty comes with a price. Many modern roses require more maintenance than old roses or species roses because they aren't as cold-hardy or disease-resistant.

HYBRID TEAS

For most people, a rose means a hybrid tea rose. These roses bear long, narrow, high-center buds, one per stem. The canes are often bare at the base, which makes hybrid teas best suited to mixed borders, herb gardens, and perennial beds where lower-growing plants can hide their gawky legs. Hybrid teas grow 3 to 5 feet high.

- Flower continually throughout the growing season
- Are available in all rose colors
- The flower form is usually semidouble or double.
- Hardiness, disease resistance, and fragrance vary greatly from cultivar to cultivar.
- Hardy only to Zone 8, so winter protection is a must
- Need rich soil, plenty of fertilizer, and ample water
- Hard pruning is required to encourage new growth and abundant flowering.

Hybrid tea roses, including 'Pink Favorite', fill the garden with blooms from summer through fall.

FUN FACT

OLD ROSES ARE ROSES THAT WERE BRED BEFORE 1867, THE DATE WHEN THE FIRST HYBRID TEA ROSE WAS INTRODUCED. THE DEBUT OF HYBRID TEAS MARKS THE START OF THE MODERN ERA OF ROSE BREEDING.

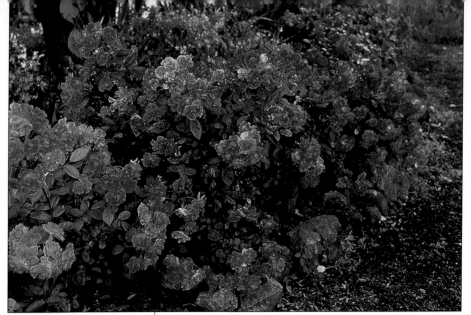

Packed with 1½-inch, medium pink flowers from summer to fall, 'China Doll' requires very little maintenance—an exceptional trait of polyantha roses.

POLYANTHAS

Polyanthas are bushy, 2-foot-tall plants with finely textured leaves. They're sturdy, trouble-free plants, so they're good choices for massing, edgings, and hedges.

- Produce clusters of small (1-inch) single, semidouble, or double flowers all season

- Generally hardy to Zone 5

- Bloom in shades of pink, white, red, orange, or yellow

- Need little pruning, except to remove dead or diseased wood or to shape the plants

- The Latin word *polyantha* means "many-flowered."

- Plant low-growing polyanthas around the base of taller floribundas and grandifloras for multitudes of blooms.

- Deadhead up to a month before frost for constant color.

- Good choice for small gardens

FLORIBUNDAS

A result of cross-breeding polyanthas with hybrid tea roses, floribundas are bushy plants that grow 2 to 4 feet tall. They're excellent for low hedges and mass plantings as well as specimens in flower borders.

- Bear many flowers per stem throughout the growing season

- Flowers are larger than polyantha blooms and about half the size of hybrid tea roses.

- Flowers can be single, semidouble, or double and come in the entire color range for roses.

- Generally hardy to Zone 6

- Need pruning to maintain their shape; to remove weak, dead, or old wood; and to remove faded flowers

- Many of the floribundas are disease-resistant—check varieties before choosing.

- Need rich, well-drained soil

One of the taller floribundas, 'Anisley Dickson', also called simply 'Dicky', reaches a height of 4 feet and bears 3-inch salmon blooms.

FUN FACT

THE "TEXAS ROSE RUSTLERS" ARE NOT A GROUP OF PLANT THIEVES, BUT AN ORGANIZATION OF OLD ROSE ENTHUSIASTS IN TEXAS. THEY SEARCH OUT OLD ROSE VARIETIES IN CEMETERIES AND FARMSTEADS AND, IF GIVEN PERMISSION, TAKE CUTTINGS IN ORDER TO PROPAGATE THE OLD VARIETIES.

The bicolor pink and yellow blooms of 'Sundowner' are the typical shape of a hybrid tea rose, but because this shrub is a grandiflora, it bears dozens of blooms at a time.

quick tip

Where you live will influence how tall your rose plant will grow. Southern gardeners who have long, warm growing conditions will have larger plants than rose growers in the Midwest and Northeast who have shorter growing seasons.

GRANDIFLORAS

A result of crossing hybrid tea roses with floribundas, grandifloras combine the classic hybrid tea rose flower form with the floriferous bloom habit of floribundas. Grandifloras generally grow 4 to 6 feet—and sometimes even taller. Because they're so tall, grandifloras work best at the back of flowerbeds or shrub borders.

- The high-centered flowers are borne singly or in clusters on long stems.
- Generally hardy to Zone 6
- Bloom continuously all season
- Flowers are generally semidouble or double and come in all rose colors; fragrance depends on the cultivar.
- A good choice for cut arrangements
- Most grandifloras are disease-resistant.
- Deadhead up to a month before frost for lots of repeat bloom.
- Cut back healthy canes by one-half to one-third for vigorous flower production.

It's hard to tell miniature roses such as these 'Little Jackie' minis apart from their larger relatives here, but these dainty blossoms are only half the size of the 'Sundowner' grandifloras pictured on the opposite page.

MINIATURES

Every aspect of miniature roses is reduced in size, including the stems, leaves, and flowers. The flowers can be single, semidouble, or double. Miniature roses can also be raised as houseplants, although you need a great deal of light to get them to bloom indoors.

- Bloom about one month earlier than shrub roses

- Hardy to Zone 5

- Need pruning to remove dead wood, to thin, or to improve shape

- Generally from 10 to 18 inches tall, miniatures come in a variety of forms— trailing, cascading, and climbing.

- Ideal for container plantings, hanging baskets, rock gardens, and as edging in mixed borders

- For long-blooming color in a small area, plant a group of miniatures spaced about 18 inches apart.

quick tip

Roses planted in containers will need protection from winter cold. Dig a hole in a protected spot in the garden and "plant" the container for winter. Mulch the top with leaves.

A CLOSER LOOK AT ROSE FLOWERS

ROSE FLOWERS vary from one type of plant to another in type, color, and shape. Rose growers and horticulturists use special terms to describe the differences between flowers. Here's a summary of what those terms mean.

Flower Fullness

Single: 5 to 7 petals in a single row

Semidouble: 8 to 20 petals in two or three rows

Moderately full double: 21 to 29 petals in three or four rows

Full double: 30 to 39 petals in four or more rows

Very full double: 40 or more petals in numerous rows

Flower Colors

Single: Similar color throughout

Bicolor: The reverse, or back, distinctly different in color from the front

Blend: Two or more distinct colors on the front of each petal

Striped: Two or more distinct colors on each petal, with at least one in distinct stripes or bands

'Attissimo' bears velvety red single flowers.

'Morning Star' is a semidouble, bicolor rose.

Flower Shapes

Button center: A round green center or eye in a fully open rose bloom, formed in very double roses

Globular: Very full double flower with petals curving inward, with a round or globelike shape

Open center: Single, semidouble, or double flower with a stamen that's prominent when the flower is fully open

Open-cupped: Semidouble or double flower, with a distinctly rounded, cuplike shape

Pompon: Very full double flower with short petals evenly arranged into a rounded bloom

Quartered center: Inner petals folded into three, four, or five distinct sections (or quarters) when the flower is fully open

Reflexed: Outer petals curve backward as they open

Rosette: A double flower with short petals evenly arranged into a flat, low-centered bloom

Saucer: Single, semidouble, or double flower with outer petals curving slightly upward in a saucerlike shape

'Heritage', an old English rose, displays a quartered center.

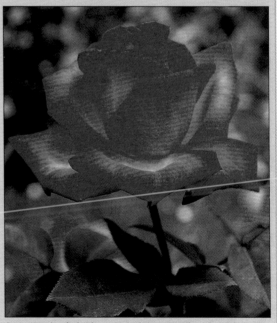

'Signature', a hybrid tea rose, features reflexed petals.

NARROWING YOUR CHOICES

Once you've decided whether to plant a species rose, old rose, or some type of modern rose, you've taken the first step. However, you still need to decide on a partic-ular species or cultivar. You can narrow your selection by focusing on the flowers. Do you have favorites? Is a rose only a rose to you if it's a double red? Or do you want a particular color to go with other flowers or features? For instance, a yellow, white, or peach rose might look better in front of an orange brick wall than a red or pink rose.

Color and Form

- Species and old roses tend more toward shades of pink, white, and mauve.

- Species and old rose flowers range from flat single or semidouble to many-petaled doubles that are open-cupped, globular, or quartered.

- Newer hybrids include many more reds, oranges, yellows, pinks, whites, and bicolors.

- Modern rose flowers have high centers with long inner petals forming a prominent central cone that rises from a flatter cup of outer petals.

Fragrance

Fragrance is another important aspect of roses, whether you're enjoying them indoors or outside in the garden. Although it's generally true that the older types of roses seem more fragrant than newer roses, many newer cultivars have a delightful fragrance, and there are old roses without a trace of fragrance. Fortu-nately, fragrance seems to be back on the rose breeder's agenda, so we can look forward to more new roses that "smell like a rose."

If you'll be using your roses for potpourri or other scented crafts, alba, Bourbon, damask, moss, musk, and rugosa roses all make good choices.

CHOOSING ROSES FOR LOW MAINTENANCE

Beyond their appearance and fragrance, you'll want to keep low maintenance in mind when you choose your roses. Look to the shrub roses first for trouble-free growing, especially the rugosas (species roses), polyanthas, and Meidiland roses. Then consider the hardy, pest-resistant cultivars of the old garden roses, the species roses, and the most pest- and disease-resistant of the modern hybrid teas, floribundas, grandifloras, and miniatures. You'll find some of the best choices for specific situations starting on page 18.

This pink Meidiland rose is just one of dozens of practically care-free shrub roses that you can choose from for a low-maintenance addition to your garden.

FINALIZING THE DECISION

ONCE YOU KNOW how you'll use your rose, you still need to decide which is the "best" plant for the purpose. Fortunately, you can find any number of roses to suit virtually every site in your landscape. To help you to wade through the choices, look at more than just the flower—consider the following:

- How long is the blooming season?
- Does the rose have showy hips (seedpods) to extend its season of interest?
- How does the plant look when it isn't in bloom?
- Will it blend with the surrounding colors, shapes, and textures?
- How much maintenance does it require?
- Is it fragrant? Is fragrance important in your chosen site?
- Is it disease-resistant?

DISEASE-RESISTANT ROSES

The easiest way to cut down on rose maintenance is to start by planting roses that are resistant to pests and diseases. We've divided the disease-resistant roses into groups so you can easily find the type you need for your landscaping purposes. Simply find the heading you're looking for and you'll have your roses at a glance. You don't have to limit your choices to these lists—they're just a starting point for buying disease-resistant roses.

Shrub and Groundcover Roses

The term *shrub rose* is a catch-all designation that the American Rose Society has created to include a large variety of hardy, easy-to-grow shrubs. They range in size from groundcovers to 12-foot-tall giants! They're known as low-maintenance landscaping roses and most are attractive both in and out of bloom. Look to this group for the largest number of disease-resistant varieties. Some of the best shrub roses for garden use include David Austin roses, Buck hybrids, Meidiland roses, and the newly introduced Parkland and Explorer series from Canada. Here are just a few of the many reliable varieties of groundcover and shrub roses.

'Carefree Wonder': Clusters of double, deep pink flowers that bloom continuously on shrubs that grow 5 feet tall × 3 feet wide (Zones 4–9)

'John Davis': Large clusters of scented, double, pink flowers on

'Sarah van Fleet', a shrub rose, can grow quite large, especially in a warm climate. To keep it under control, don't overfertilize. It fills in nicely against a brick wall, and it's also perfect for the back of a shrub or perennial border.

arching canes that reach to 6 feet—best as a trailing shrub or tall climber; very cold hardy (Zones 3–9)

'Knock Out': Scented, deep cherry red flower clusters on a rounded shrub 3 feet tall × 3 feet wide. (Zones 4–9)

'Sarah van Fleet': Sweet, clove-scented pink flowers on upright to arching canes; reaches maximum size of 8 feet × 5 feet wide (Zones 3–9)

'Scarlet Meidiland': Mounding trailing habit; canes grow to 3 feet tall × 6 feet wide; provides good repeat bloom (Zones 4–9)

'Sea Foam': Low-spreading shrub with long-blooming clusters of double, creamy white flowers; vigorous and prostrate, plants grow 3 feet tall × 6 feet wide (Zones 4–9)

Miniature Roses

Although there are many minis to choose from, many are susceptible to diseases. Here are some that are exceptionally disease-resistant. (*Note:* Most miniature roses are hardy to Zone 5.)

'Baby Diana': An orange bloomer

'Black Jade': Double, dark red, velvety flowers

'Jackie': Climber with fragrant, light yellow blooms

'Magic Carousel': 30-inch shrub with double, white flowers edged with red

'Rainbow's End': Readily available cultivar with yellow blooms edged with red

'Starina': Fragrant, bright red and orange flowers

> **quick tip**
>
> If you want a splash of summer color, grow a group of roses together. Use all one cultivar rather than mixing them so you don't dilute the effect. Three to five bushes is usually enough to create quite an impact. Choose a repeat-bloomer for a long season of color.

'Rainbow's End' is a standout mini. It's hardy and disease-resistant and puts on a show of colorful blooms that change from yellow edged in red to orange-red at their finish.

'Frau Dagmar Hastrup' sports clove-scented, light pink flowers on a sturdy shrub with a spreading habit.

A casual cottage garden is a perfect spot for 'La Marne', one of the taller polyantha roses. Here it flanks an entryway, but it also works well in the back of a flower border.

Rugosa Roses and Their Hybrids

Both the straight species, *Rosa rugosa,* and its many cultivars are known for their disease resistance. Here are some of the finest varieties and cultivars.

***Rosa rugosa* var. *rubra*:** Large, single, magenta-purple flowers and large, showy hips (Zones 2–9)

Rugosa hybrid 'Blanc double de Courbet': Fragrant, semi-double, white flowers and showy hips on a 4- to 5-foot shrub (Zones 4–9)

'F.J. Grootendorst': Bears unscented, bright red, fringed flowers that resemble carnations; foliage turns orange-red in autumn (Zones 4–8)

'Frau Dagmar Hastrup': Compact shrub about 3 feet tall × 3 feet wide that produces large, single, silver-pink flowers and tomato-red hips (Zones 4–9)

'Hansa': Reaches 6 to 7 feet in height and has semi-double, purple-red flowers and orange-red hips (Zones 4–9)

Polyantha Roses

The bushy, fine-textured polyanthas have a well-deserved reputation for being trouble-free. Some noteworthy choices follow.

'Cecile Brunner': 3-foot-tall bush with fragrant, pale pink flowers; also available as a climbing cultivar (Zones 5–9)

'China Doll': 2-foot-tall bush with double, pink flowers and bright green, disease-resistant leaves (Zones 5–9)

'La Marne': 5-foot-tall bush with masses of pink-and-white, cupped, and ruffled flowers (Zones 5–9)

'The Fairy': 2-foot-tall bush with abundant sprays of small, double, light pink flowers (Zones 5–9)

Ramblers and Climbers

'America': 8- to 10-foot climber with large, salmon-colored, hybrid-tea–type flowers and a bushy habit (Zones 5–9)

'Alchymist': 8- to 12-foot-tall arching shrub with heavy canes and large, fragrant, yellow and apricot flowers; doesn't rebloom but is very striking in early summer (Zones 5–9)

'Alchymist' has gorgeous blossoms and a wonderful scent. It's not a rebloomer, but its dark green, glossy leaves are disease-resistant, so it looks attractive even after the blossoms fade.

'Climbing Cecile Brunner': Can climb to 20 feet; fragrant, pale pink flowers (Zones 6–9)

'Dortmund': Showy red climber that forms clusters of large, single flowers and orange-red hips if not deadheaded (Zones 5–9)

'Dublin Bay': Repeat-blooming, large, double, red flowers (Zones 5–9)

'New Dawn': Blooms heavily in early summer with large, fragrant, pearly pink to white flowers; has a second blooming in late summer (Zones 5–9)

If you love red roses, the large, lush, velvety red blooms of 'Crimson Bouquet' are for you!

Hybrid Teas and Grandifloras

Even disease-resistant hybrid tea and grandiflora roses require a lot of maintenance compared to self-reliant shrub roses or polyanthas. However, disease resistance is a priority with breeders, so every year the organic grower has more choices.

'Crimson Bouquet': $4\frac{1}{2}$-foot-tall grandiflora that bears scented, blood red blooms (Zone 4b)

'Gemini': Double, creamy pink flowers on a vigorous $5\frac{1}{2}$-foot-tall bush (Zone 5)

'Keepsake': 5-foot-tall bush with very fragrant, double, high-centered, multishaded pink flowers, borne singly and in clusters, and glossy leaves on dense, sturdy canes (Zones 5–9)

'Mrs. Dudley Cross': Thornless, 3- to 4-foot-high leafy tea rose; creamy yellow, pink-edged flowers (Zones 7–9)

'Pink Parfait': 4-foot-tall grandiflora with prolific, double, pink flowers (Zone 6)

'Pink Peace': 5-foot-tall bush with very fragrant, very double, high-centered, deep pink flowers and disease-resistant, leathery leaves (Zones 6–9)

'Queen Elizabeth': Bears double, clear pink flowers continuously on 5- to 6-foot-tall shrubs (Zone 6–9)

Floribunda Roses

When it comes to the best floribundas, here are some of the experts' picks for good disease resistance.

'Betty Prior': Continuously bears single carmine pink flowers on 4-foot-tall shrubs (Zones 5–9)

'Europeana': One of the best dark red, ever-blooming floribunda roses; bears large clusters of double, deep red flowers on dense, 3-foot-tall shrubs (Zones 6–9)

'Nearly Wild': Resembles a species rose with its continuously blooming sprays of single, clear pink flowers; upright, rounded shrubs grow to 4 feet tall (Zones 4–9)

'Sunsprite': 2- to 4-foot-tall shrub with fragrant, double, golden yellow flowers (Zones 5–9)

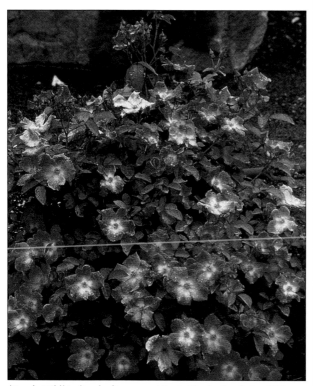

'Nearly Wild' isn't only disease-resistant, it's also hardy to -40°F (Zone 3), making it a good choice for northern gardeners.

CHOOSING THE RIGHT SPOT

WITH SO MANY roses available, you can see how choosing the perfect one isn't easy. Ask yourself, "What do I want roses to do for my landscape?" To answer the question, go into your yard and examine your potential sites. You may want to look for the following:

- Areas that get *at least* six hours of sun a day

- Existing perennial or shrub borders that could be improved with roses

- Views that you'd like to screen with a privacy hedge of roses

- Bare walls, fences, pillars, stumps, or even eyesores that could be used to support a climber

- Sunny slopes in need of groundcover

- Potential sites for an arbor, trellis, or pergola

GRAFTS AND ROOTSTOCKS

MOST ROSES available today are *grafted*. Grafting involves removing a bud from the stem of the rose cultivar you want to grow and implanting it on the stem of another type or cultivar of rose (called the rootstock), which provides the root system for the new plant. From the propagator's point of view, this is done mainly for convenience. Grafting is a fast, efficient way to propagate large numbers of roses, and to quickly introduce new varieties.

Although there's no conclusive evidence, most breeders believe that roses that haven't been grafted (called own-root roses) are often hardier than grafted ones. This is definitely true in cold-climate areas like New England, the Great Lakes region, and much of Canada.

Some rose growers specialize in own-root roses and sell only cutting-propagated plants. If you live in Zone 4 or north, you may want to seek out a mail-order nursery that features such plants.

Species Roses

Straight species roses are generally problem-free if grown in conditions that mimic their native habitat. Although not easily found in the market, they can be useful in the landscape. (See "Recommended Reading & Resources" on page 99 for mail-order information.)

Chestnut rose (*Rosa roxburghii*): Bears bright pink, 2-inch flowers on a 6-foot plant; has attractive peeling bark and showy hips (Zones 6–9)

Swamp rose (*R. palustris*): A suckering plant that produces fragrant, single, pink blooms in late June to early July (depending on region) and orange-red hips later in the season (Zones 3–7)

Virginia rose (*R. virginiana*): A suckering 3- to 5-foot shrub that produces single, pink flowers in June (depending on region) and red hips, which ripen in late summer (Zones 3–7)

The 3-inch blooms of this chestnut rose combined with the attractive bark and hips make this species rose a real showstopper. But you need room for it to grow to its mature size of 6 × 6 feet.

COLD-HARDY ROSES

In areas where winters are very cold, many roses won't make it to spring. Fortunately, there are choices even for the Zone 3 gardener. Species roses, such as *Rosa glauca* and *R. rugosa* are hardy to Zone 2. Many *R. rugosa* cultivars are also cold-hardy and can survive in Zone 3. The Explorer series and the Parkland series of roses bred in Canada are hardy to -40°F. Some choices from these series follow.

'Champlain': 3-foot-tall shrub with prolific, bright red blooms (Zones 3–9)

'John Cabot': Prolific climber with fuchsia flowers (Zones 3–9)

'Morden Centennial': Well-shaped, 5-foot-tall shrub, covered with fragrant, deep pink blooms in late June and early July (Zones 2–9)

'Simon Fraser': 2½-foot shrub with masses of semi-double, pink flowers throughout the summer (Zones 3–9)

Some rose species are also very cold-hardy. *R. rugosa, R. setigera, R. spinosissima,* and many of their cultivars also survive frigid winters. Here are two good examples.

'Frau Dagmar Hartopp': 3-foot shrub with large, single, silver-pink blooms and red hips (Zones 4-9)

'Wiliam Baffin': Repeat bloomer; deep pink blooms on arching, 8-foot canes (Zones 2–9)

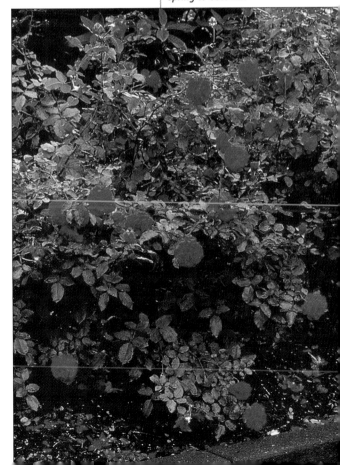

'Champlain', one of the Explorer series roses, bears dozens of 2½- to 3-inch red blossoms from spring to autumn.

*Yellow Lady Banks rose (*Rosa banksiae *var.* lutea) *is only hardy to 10°F, so it's not a great choice for northern gardeners, but it sure can stand up to the heat of southern gardens.*

HEAT-TOLERANT ROSES

Many roses stop blooming and start mildewing during long bouts of humid, moist heat. Here are some roses that can take the heat.

'Champney's Pink Cluster': Continuously blooming clusters of small, double, pink flowers on 4-foot shrubs (Zones 6–9)

Cherokee rose (*Rosa laevigata*): Once-blooming, species rose climber with fragrant, large, single, white blooms (Zones 7–9)

China roses: Generally hardy to 0°F, these old roses are good choices for Zones 7–10; include 'Old Blush', a 6-foot bush with light pink flowers, and 'Archduke Charles', a 3-foot bush with rose red flowers

Lady Banks rose (*R. banksiae* var. *albo-plena*): Hardy to 10°F; 20-foot climber with small, fragrant, double, white or yellow blooms (Zone 8)

'Queen Elizabeth': Clear pink blooms on a 6-foot-tall grandiflora (Zones 5–9)

FRAGRANT ROSES

While old roses are known for their wonderful fragrance, many hybrid tea roses are also bred for fragrance. Here are a few *relatively* disease-resistant choices.

'Chrysler Imperial': Deep crimson flowers on a 3½-foot bush; susceptible to mildew and blackspot in cool, wet weather (Zones 4–9)

'Fragrant Cloud': Repeat-blooming bush with coral-red flowers; vigorous; susceptible to disease (Zones 5–9)

'Mister Lincoln': Double, dark red, repeating blooms on erect canes (Zones 5–9)

Moss roses—named for the mossy, resinous growth covering the outside of flower buds—are usually very fragrant. Examples of these old roses follow.

'Communis': 4-foot bush with very fragrant, once-blooming, pink flowers (Zone 4)

'Henri Martin': 5-foot bush with fragrant, once-blooming, double, crimson flowers fading to deep rose (Zones 4–8)

'White Bath': 4-foot bush with very fragrant, white flowers (Zones 5–9)

'Chrysler Imperial' is a hybrid tea rose noted for its damask fragrance and 5-inch blooms. It's susceptible to powdery mildew, so plant it where it will have excellent air circulation.

ROSES FOR WET SITES

THE IDEAL SOIL for roses is rich in organic matter, moist, and well drained. If the spot where you've chosen to plant your roses is wetter than ideal, you can create raised beds so the soil can drain properly.

Another option is to plant a bog garden using species roses that tolerate wet sites. Swamp rose (*Rosa palustris,* Zones 3–7) and New England shining rose (*R. nitida,* Zones 3–7) both thrive in these conditions, where they can be combined with other moisture-loving perennials and shrubs. Sedges and rushes, primroses, blue flag iris (*Iris versicolor*), winterberry holly (*Ilex verticillata*), and summersweet (*Clethra alnifolia*) are just a few of the many attractive bog garden choices that you can plant with your roses.

Good quality bypass pruners and a pair of heavy-duty gloves are two of the most useful items you can own as a rose gardener.

chapter three

Tools & Supplies for Growing Roses

Taking care of roses doesn't require a lot of specialty tools, but having the right tool for the job does make planting, pruning, and watering easier. In this chapter you'll find all the tools you need to get your roses growing and tips to keep them in fine form.

7 ESSENTIAL TOOLS FOR ROSE GARDENING

To plant and care for roses, you'll need some basic tools to help make your job easier.

Shovel or spade. Use this to dig planting holes and to shovel on the mulch, manure, or compost.

Pruning shears. Invest in a quality pair of pruning shears to make it easier to cut back roses and lessen the chance of disease problems.

Gloves. Roses are thorny, so avoid snags and scratches by wearing a pair of heavy-duty gloves.

Lopping shears or pruning saw. If you grow climbing or rambling roses, use one of these to extend your reach and easily cut through the thicker canes.

Ties or staples. More stuff for climbing roses. Climbers can get heavy and will need supports to grow on. You'll need to tie them to supports or staple them to stone walls.

Pegs. If a rose groundcover is your dream, land-scape staples or wooden pegs will make it easy to hold flexible canes in place low to the ground to create the look you desire.

Fertilizer. To ensure a season of beautiful blooms, you'll want to feed your roses with organic fertilizers.

> Invest in a quality pair of pruning shears to make it easier to cut back roses and lessen the chance of disease problems.

PLANTING TOOLS

When it comes to planting roses, you probably already have what you need in your garage or shed.

Shovels and Spades

To dig planting holes, you can use either an all-purpose shovel or a digging spade. What's the difference between the two? Both come with blades of varying widths and depths. A good digging spade has a narrow, flat blade with a sharp, square edge and a handle that's 28 to 32 inches long. A shovel has a more rounded blade that comes to a point, and the handle is generally 4 feet long.

Shovel

Spade

quick tip

When buying a shovel or spade, look for one made of forged steel with a white ash or fiberglass handle. You'll also want a turned edge, or footrest, on the shoulders of the blade to protect your foot when you put your weight down on it.

Stakes

Planting time is also, in some cases, staking time. If you're planting a standard (tree) rose, you'll need to drive a support stake into the ground next to the plant. (To learn more about caring for a standard rose, see page 83.) Bamboo stakes are good because they're inexpensive, flexible, and inconspicuous. You can also choose wood, metal, or plastic stakes. Make sure that the stake is long enough to reach the bud union where the rose is grafted onto the standard. It's also a good idea to choose a stake that will blend in with the standard. Bright green or another color will draw attention away from the rose blooms.

PRUNING TOOLS

Pruning may not be your favorite part of growing roses, but it can certainly go quickly and smoothly when you have good equipment that's comfortable to use. Compare the workmanship of various brands and the way the tools feel in your hand before you buy.

To get the job done right, you'll need to have the following tools on hand.

Gloves

To avoid a painful experience, choose a thornproof pair of gloves, preferably ones that cover your wrists for better protection. Leather (cowhide, goatskin, or pigskin) gloves work well, as do rubber- and plastic-coated gloves.

quick tip

A leather holster to carry your pruners is a wise investment. It makes a handy carrier for toting your shears with you as you stroll through the garden, and it won't tear the way your pants pocket would.

Rubber-coated gloves

Leather gloves

Hand-Pruning Shears

Be kind to your canes and use bypass pruners that have blades that work like scissors, rather than anvil-type pruners, which have a sharp blade that closes against a metal plate. Because pruning shears are the most essential tool you'll own, buy a good-quality pair, preferably one for which replacement parts are available. Keep the cutting edges sharp and the parts clean and lubricated (wipe them with an oiled cloth after each use), and your pruners will serve you for many years.

Bypass pruners

Lopping Shears

Lopping shears are essentially long-handled pruning shears. The extra handle length increases your reach and gives you leverage for cutting branches that are finger-size and larger in diameter.

Lopping shears

Pruning Saw

If you have mature climbing roses, a pruning saw is a necessity—it's great for sawing through canes over 2 inches in diameter. Otherwise, you probably won't need one. (Well, at least not for your roses.) Pruning saws are small hand saws with a replaceable blade that's about 6 inches long. Folding models are available, which makes them easy—and safe—to fit in your pocket.

Unlike carpenter's saws, pruning saws are designed to cut as you pull the blade toward you, rather than as you push it away. So, when you take your pruning saw to be sharpened, make sure the person sharpening it is aware of this so your saw comes back sharpened, not ruined.

Folding pruning saw

TRAINING TOOLS AND STRUCTURES

Climbing roses can be left to scramble into trees and shrubs or to hang over retaining walls. Or, for a more classical look, you can train climbers onto trellises, fences, arbors, pergolas, posts, or pillars.

Structures

When purchasing or constructing wooden trellises or arbors, look for sturdy wood posts sized from 1 × ½ inch up to 2 inches square. If you aren't using rot-resistant wood like recycled redwood or red cedar, treat it with a borax-based wood preservative, which is safe for plants and the environment.

A white wooden trellis against a light-color house makes an inconspicuous yet sturdy support for a 'Climbing Cécile Brunner' rose.

ARBOR AND TRELLIS IDEAS

ALTHOUGH MANY attractive structures are available in stores and catalogs, you don't have to limit yourself to these choices. You can make your own strong, long-lasting support structures from wood, metal, or sturdy plastic pipe (such as PVC). Cedar posts make good rot-resistant pillars.

Also, keep an eye out for found materials that can function as support structures, such as an old wrought-iron gate or fence section, or wooden ladders that you can purchase at a flea market to incorporate into your landscape. Existing wire and wooden fences, lampposts, porch columns, outbuilding walls, and crabapple trees all make interesting supports for climbing roses, too. Think creatively—the possibilities are endless.

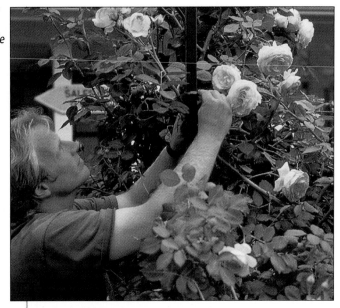

To create a romantic look of a rose-covered arch, you'll need to give the roses a little help. Use inconspicuous ties such as the green plastic ones shown here to train your roses to grow where you want them without damaging their canes.

If you prefer a low-growing groundcover to climbing roses, train flexible-caned roses to hug the ground by bending the canes and pinning them in place with landscape staples or pins you make yourself from wire.

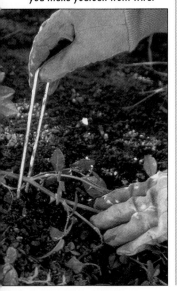

Ties and Staples

Climbing roses use their thorns to cling onto natural trellises such as trees and shrubs. But if you're using manmade supports, you'll need to attach the roses to the supports—either with ties or staples. To tie rose canes to trellises, use plastic or rubber-coated wire, raffia, or thin nylon cord to make a figure eight between the cane and the trellis so the tie won't cut into the cane. Some gardeners prefer jute twine because it's an organic fiber flexible enough to allow the canes to expand as they grow; plus, it's biodegradable.

For attaching canes to walls or posts, use fencing staples as fastening points, hammered in at about 4-inch intervals.

Pins and Pegs

Roses can climb high—or they can lay low. To create a rose groundcover on a sunny slope, peg the arching canes to the ground with wire pins or wooden stakes. If you use wire pins, make wire U-shaped staples that look like giant hairpins, and pin the rose canes to the ground. For pegs, you can use 1½-foot lengths of ¾-inch-diameter broom handles. Drill a hole near the top of the peg, pound the undrilled end into the ground, and anchor the cane to the ground by tying it with cord threaded through the hole.

FERTILIZER

No single magic fertilizing formula works for all climates, all soils, all conditions, or all roses. Knowing your soil conditions will help you determine what type of fertilizer you should treat your roses to and how much. You can learn more about testing your soil for nutrients, pH level, and drainage (which is critical for roses) by reading "Preparing the Soil" on page 43. Then, for specifics on what type of fertilizers to keep on hand, and how often to apply them, see "Feeding Roses Naturally" on page 56.

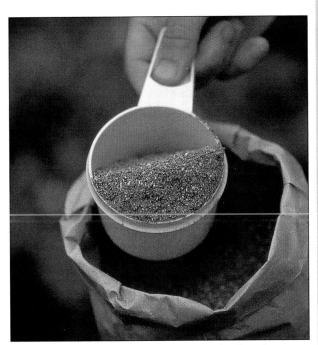

Alfalfa meal is one of the most popular organic fertilizers for rose growers because it's so high in nitrogen—a nutrient that every hungry rose needs.

FLOWER-ARRANGING TOOLS

IF YOU PLAN to cut some of your roses to bring them indoors to enjoy, you may want to add a few more tools and supplies to your shopping list.

In the not-necessary-but-nice-to-have category are floral foam, wire, and scissors. Floral foam, sold in blocks, holds large amounts of water and anchors your arrangement. Floral wire is used to reinforce stems and make corsages. You can buy special short-bladed floral scissors or use high-quality stainless steel household scissors to cleanly cut thin, nonwoody rose stems.

Thornstrippers, or stem strippers—inexpensive gadgets that remove thorns and leaves from long rose stems—are good to have if you plan on handling a lot of roses.

Planting rosebushes isn't hard, as long as you know when to plant and how deep to plant—and as long as you prepare the soil properly beforehand.

chapter four

Buying &
Planting Roses

Learn how to shop for the best-quality roses (not necessarily the most expensive!) and how to get those roses off to a good start. Planting roses right gives them a real head start in the garden, whether you start with container-grown or bareroot plants.

GARDEN CENTER SHOPPING TIPS

Most roses are sold as grafted plants. They're grown for two years in fields, then dug up in the fall and placed in cold storage.

From there, they may be shipped as bareroot plants from mail-order suppliers, packaged as bare-root plants for sale in stores, or sold to nurseries to be potted into containers for sale.

Buying roses at garden centers, nurseries, and other local outlets gives you the advantages of getting roses when you want them and seeing exactly what you're getting. Although the selection of roses is much smaller than when you buy by mail, many people prefer buying at least some of their roses this way. Both dormant plants and container-grown plants that have leafed out (many of which are flowering) are available. To get the most for your money, follow these buying tips.

Buying roses at garden centers, nurseries, and other local outlets gives you the advantages of getting roses when you want them and seeing exactly what you're getting.

- Buy plants as early as possible to get the best selection, but be sure to wait until it's time to plant in your area. (See "Regional Rose-Planting Guide" on page 40 if you're not sure.)
- To avoid buying on impulse, make a list of what you want ahead of time.

These semidormant roses don't have the appeal of those with a flush of bloom, but buying them at this stage will assure you a larger selection. Plus, you'll get to enjoy their full season of bloom in your own garden.

- If you find a cultivar you like but aren't familiar with, write down the name and go home and read about it rather than buying it on the spot.

- Dormant plants should be labeled as to grade (see "Going by the Numbers" on the opposite page). It's best if they are completely dormant, with no leaf buds beginning to open.

- Buy healthy container-grown roses that are clearly labeled. A healthy plant will have sturdy stems with rich green leaves—free from disease and insects.

- The soil in the container should be moist.

- Signs of trouble in a container-grown plant include wilted leaves, weeds growing in the pot, dry soil, signs of insects or disease, split pot, thick roots growing through the base of the pot, and lopsided growth. Don't buy plants with these conditions.

- Ask about replacement guarantees, and always keep your receipt.

SMART MAIL-ORDER SHOPPING

With thousands of rose cultivars available, not even the best local garden centers and nurseries can begin to carry more than a comparative handful. Mail-order nurseries fill a critical need because they can maintain a much larger range of stock for sale. If you buy from mail-order companies, you should be able to find every rose you'd like to grow. Most mail-order companies are very reliable, but even with the best, it's important to know exactly what they're offering. Here are some tips for getting the most from mail-order shopping.

- Whenever possible, use companies that other gardeners recommend.

- Be wary of companies that make outrageous claims or have prices that are far below those in other catalogs.

- Compare descriptions of rose cultivars in various catalogs and rose books. If possible, visit gardens where you can see the roses you're interested in before buying them.

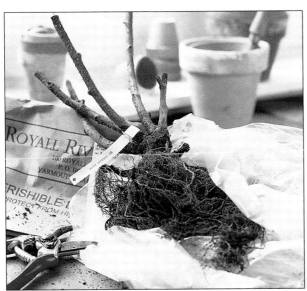

Mail-order bareroot roses should arrive with no new growth starting to sprout. Get them in the soil before leaves start to emerge.

GOING BY THE NUMBERS

ROSES ARE generally field-grown for two years before being sold. Roses grown and sold as two-year-old, grafted, field-grown plants are graded No. 1, No. 1½, or No. 2 and should be labeled as such. But what do these numbers mean?

A No. 1 plant is the best quality and will provide you with the strongest growth and most bloom, during the first year and succeeding years.

You can recognize a No. 1 plant because it will have three or more healthy canes that are each at least ½ inch in diameter and 6 inches long. Number 1½ plants have fewer and smaller canes, but with a little extra effort, they'll produce good growth. Avoid No. 2 plants because they require a great deal of tender loving care to get them to measure up.

REGIONAL ROSE-PLANTING GUIDE

USE THESE guidelines, based on where you live, to determine when you should buy and plant roses.

Pacific and Gulf Coast:
December to January

Inland Pacific Coast, Southwest, and mid-South:
January to February

Upper South and Mid-Atlantic coast:
March to April

Lower mountain elevations and lower Midwest:
April

Mid-mountain elevations, Plains, upper Midwest, and lower Northeast:
April to May

Higher mountain elevations, northern Plains, and upper Northeast:
May

● Read the introduction to the catalog and the order blank. The best suppliers give specifics on the size, age, and grade of the roses, shipping information, whether the plants are own-root or grafted, replacement guarantees, and substitution policies.

● Learn to read between the lines of rose descriptions. Because catalog writers are trying to sell their products, descriptions can be misleading—for example, "light scent" usually means the rose has hardly any fragrance. And "exhibition-quality" flowers may be great for rose shows, but the plants may not look good in the landscape. Seldom are plants quite as glorious, hardy, or disease-resistant as described. If some of the descriptions are honest about the pitfalls of given cultivars, then you'll know that the more extravagant claims are probably fairly accurate as well.

● Don't be so overcome by what's in the catalog description that you don't see what's missing. If you don't see "fragrant," "disease-resistant," "attractive foliage," "reblooms," and other desirable qualities, it may be that the rose doesn't have them.

● For the best selection, order early. Many smaller growers have limited quantities, especially of unusual cultivars, and popular ones can sell out quickly.

WHEN TO BUY AND PLANT ROSES

To have the rose cultivars you want, it's best to buy them early. When you shop locally, wait to buy dormant plants until the proper planting time in your area. Buying bareroot roses late in the spring means the top growth has started without a well-established root system; plants are likely to succumb to hot, dry weather unless you give the proper care. Container-grown roses are often put on sale in summer and early fall, but by that time they are potbound and require special care to survive.

It's best to plant your roses soon after you buy them, whether they're bareroot or container-grown. If you have to wait a few days, however, make sure to keep bareroot roses moist and cool. Keep container-grown roses in the same amount of light as they were at the nursery, and keep the soil moist.

WHERE TO PLANT

Although roses are highly adaptable, they grow and bloom best if you give them the best conditions possible. When deciding where to plant your roses, take the following factors into consideration: soil, sunlight, water, humidity and air circulation, extreme temperatures, and accessibility.

Soil. The ideal soil for roses is slightly acidic (6.0 to 6.5 pH), rich in organic matter and nutrients, and moist but well drained—in other words, it's good garden soil. If the soil in your chosen site doesn't meet these criteria, work in lots of compost and other organic matter and correct any drainage problems.

Sunlight. Almost all roses need a site that gets at least six hours of direct sun a day to grow and bloom well. Morning sun is better than afternoon sun because dew will dry more quickly, reducing the incidence of disease.

Roses need a minimum of six hours of sunlight a day to bloom at their best, so choose an open, sunny spot such as the one that this 'Dapple Dawn' rose enjoys.

Water. Like most garden plants, roses grow best with an even supply of moisture—the equivalent of about 1 inch per week. Repeat-blooming cultivars are more dependent on steady, even moisture than species and cultivars that bloom only once a year.

Air circulation. The moisture in the air also has an effect on

Growing roses at the entryway to your home means you—and your neighbors—will get to enjoy them daily. It also means you'll be able to spot the earliest signs of pest or disease problems.

quick tip

If your whole property is shady, or if you must plant roses in a site with less than optimal light, all isn't lost. You just need to focus on roses that can make do with less. Roses that thrive with only four hours of direct sun include hybrid musks, miniatures, and most climbers.

the health of roses. Fungal diseases spread faster and do more damage in moist, stagnant conditions. If your region naturally has high humidity, grow only the most disease-resistant cultivars, or you'll find yourself applying frequent remedies and your plants will suffer. See "Disease-Resistant Roses" on page 18 for more information.

Heat and cold. Humidity isn't the only climatic factor that can affect your roses. Extremes of both heat and cold can slow growth of your roses. While cold threatens their survival, heat hampers their bloom. Choose cultivars that are recommended for your area because they'll be most tolerant of your conditions.

Easy access. The final key in siting your roses successfully is choosing locations in your yard that are easy to get to. Growing roses where you see them regularly means that you'll notice the first signs of a problem—often the difference between a quick solution and an endless battle. You'll also be able to feed and care for your plants efficiently.

PREPARING THE SOIL

Planted in the proper location and adequately maintained, a rose will live for many years. But all the care in the world won't make up for inadequate soil preparation before you plant. It makes sense to prepare the soil the best way possible so you won't end up moving the rose or struggling to help it survive.

Squeeze damp soil in your hand to determine if it's clay, loam, or sandy soil. If it holds together as the soil shown here, it's clay soil, and you'll need to improve drainage by adding compost.

Know Your Soil

The goal of preparing soil for roses is to create a planting bed that doesn't drain too quickly, yet has enough pore space so there's plenty of air for plant roots. Sandy soils have lots of air space, but they drain away water and nutrients too quickly. Clay soils, on the other hand, may have drainage problems if the proportion of clay is too high.

Clay, sand, or loam? What type of soil do you have? A fast, easy way to determine soil type is to pick up a handful of soil several days after a rain or watering. Squeeze the soil and open your hand. If the soil ball retains its shape, you have clay soil. If the soil falls apart and is gritty, you have sandy soil. If the soil partially crumbles apart you have loam—the perfect soil for growing roses!

It's important to test your soil's pH level before planting roses. If a soil test shows that the pH level is out of the 6.0 to 6.5 range, you can easily adjust it by adding soil amendments.

Soil pH. The pH level of your soil determines how well nutrients are absorbed from the water in the soil. Roses grow best with a pH of 6.0 to 6.5 (slightly acidic to near neutral). A pH test—done with a home-test kit or by your local extension service—will reveal the pH of your garden soil. (Call your local Cooperative Extension Service, listed in the blue pages of the telephone book, for information on professional soil testing.)

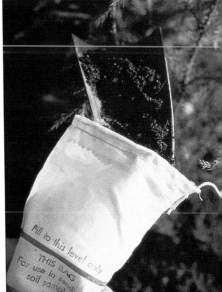

Fill to this level only

THIS BAG
For use in sending
soil sample

Getting Your Soil in Shape

Once you've learned something about your soil, what can you do about it?

1. First, prepare the soil at least several months before planting, if possible, to allow soil to settle and organic soil amendments to blend with the soil. If you need to remove grass to create a new bed for your roses, do so a season before you plant them.

2. Add organic material like rotted leaves, rotted manure, or compost to the soil. By volume, you should have one-third organic material and two-thirds soil. Use the soil you remove elsewhere in your garden, or don't remove any soil and create a raised bed.

3. Add a cupful of "magic" alfalfa meal per plant. It's high in nitrogen, it adds trace elements to the soil, and it stimulates plant growth naturally.

Balancing Soil pH

Most garden soil has an acceptable pH for growing roses, but now is the time to correct it if it isn't right. A steady diet of compost or other organic matter can gradually balance your garden soil and keep it balanced.

Dealing with Drainage

Another key soil test before planting roses is to check drainage conditions. Roses hate wet feet! Dig a hole 6 inches wide × 12 inches deep. Fill the hole with water, allow it to drain, and fill it again immediately. Again, time how long it takes the water to drain.

Using the results. If it takes six to eight hours, adding organic matter will be enough to improve soil drainage. If it takes longer than eight hours, consider growing your roses in raised beds. If your soil drains in less than six hours, adding compost is the answer. Organic matter will help hold the water in your soil.

Before you plant roses, test soil drainage by digging a hole, filling it with water, and checking to be sure the water drains away within an hour. Roses won't grow well in poorly drained soil.

PLANTING ROSES RIGHT

Container-grown roses are easier to plant than bareroot roses, but you'll have success with either type when you keep in mind the following three elements: timing, spacing, and planting depth.

Timing Is Everything

Bareroot roses are usually dormant and should be planted either in late fall or in early spring.

Container-grown roses are actively growing and can be planted any time during the growing season. However, the earlier, the better. If possible, plant in spring once frosts are over so that the roses have more time to grow in the ground—an advantage over being held in the containers, where they risk drying out, suffering nutrient deficiencies, and having their roots constricted.

Spacing Roses

Spacing requirements for roses depend on their size and use. You need enough room around each rose for

Don't plant roses too close together or you'll just be asking for trouble. Black spot and powdery mildew are more likely to crop up when air circulation isn't adequate.

CREATING RAISED BEDS

IF YOUR SOIL is extremely slow-draining, but you *really* want to grow roses, you will need to grow them in a raised bed. You can create a raised bed 6 to 12 inches high simply by mixing one-half as much organic matter as there is soil into the bed. Don't dig the soil to loosen it or remove soil from the bed.

To keep the soil from washing away, slope the sides of the bed slightly, or edge the beds with timbers, stone, or brick, depending on the style of your house and garden. Don't use wood that has been pressure-treated or treated with preservatives like creosote to border your raised beds. The chemicals in these woods can harm plants and leach into the soil.

Before setting bareroot roses in the ground, clip off any damaged or dead roots.

Set bareroot roses over a mound of soil in the planting hole, and spread the roots out.

adequate air circulation, otherwise you risk problems with powdery mildew, a plant disease that causes a white powdery film on the leaves. If you're planting more than one rose to create a mass of blooms, however, you want them close enough to create the desired effect. In general, follow these spacing guidelines.

- Hybrid teas, floribundas, and grandifloras: 24 to 30 inches apart
- Polyanthas: 18 to 24 inches apart
- Miniature, shrub, and old roses:as far apart as their mature height
- Climbers: 8 to 10 feet apart for climbing fences; 3 feet apart for climbing walls

  Note: For areas that do not get frost—or only for short periods—add 6 inches to the spacing requirements.

Planting Bareroot Roses

Choose a day when the soil is relatively dry because digging in wet soil can compact it and destroy its structure. If your bareroot roses arrive when planting conditions aren't right, you can put off planting them in the ground by planting them in containers until you—and the weather—are ready for planting. It is important, however, to get them into the soil before they're ready to sprout and grow.

Follow these steps for successful planting.

1. Set the plants in a bucket of water so the roots don't dry out during planting.

2. Prune off any damaged or dead roots, then any dead or damaged canes, cutting back to a healthy bud.

3. Dig a hole large enough for the roots to spread out naturally.

4. Make a mound of soil in the planting hole. The mound should be high enough so that the bud union (where the rose is joined to the rootstock) will be at the appropriate planting depth. See "How Deep to Plant Roses" below for specifics.

5. Set the rose on the mound, spreading out its roots.

6. Completely cover the roots with soil, tamp gently, and water well. The soil will settle and fill the hole.

Backfill the hole with the soil you removed, making sure all the roots are completely covered.

HOW DEEP TO PLANT ROSES

MOST ROSES YOU BUY will be grafted—one type of rose cultivar joined to the hearty understock of another. You can recognize these roses by the swollen or knobby area on the trunk, which is called the bud union. Most types of roses should be planted with the bud union 2 inches below the soil level to protect it from the cold. The planting depth for hybrid teas or grandifloras, however, depends on how cold it gets where you live.

Minimum Winter Temperature	Hybrid Teas and Grandifloras	All Others
32°F	1 to 2 inches above soil surface	2 inches deep
20°F	Just above soil surface	2 inches deep
Below 20°F	1 to 2 inches deep	2 inches deep

Planting Container-Grown Roses

Compared to bareroot roses, planting container-grown roses is a snap.

1. Dig a hole large enough to hold the container, making sure the top of the soil in the container is just below the ground level.

2. Tip the container and tap it to release the soil ball, or cut the container away from the rootball with a utility knife.

Remove container-grown roses carefully from the pot, tapping it to release the roots. Watch out for thorns!

3. Set the rose in the hole, holding on to the top of the rootball, rather than grasping the rose by its stem. If the rose is rootbound, loosen the rootball before planting.

4. Fill in around the rootball with soil. Water the rose, and add more soil if necessary.

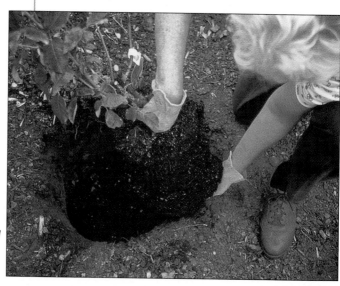

Set the rose in the planting hole so that the soil level of the plant is even with the surrounding soil.

Fill in around the rootball with soil. Here, soil is mounded in a circle around the canes to form a well so water won't run off before it can saturate the ground.

TLC FOR NEWLY PLANTED ROSES

YOUR NEW ROSES are going to need some tender loving care to get them off to a good start. Here's what you'll need to do.

- Mound 6 to 8 inches of soil around the base of each plant to prevent the canes of newly planted roses from drying out in warm, windy weather.

- If you plant roses in the fall in an area where winter temperatures dip below freezing, provide winter protection, referring to "Winter Care for Your Roses" on page 62.

- When new growth is 1 to 2 inches long, wash the soil mound away with gently flowing water, but don't blast it off with the hose.

- Check plants once or twice a week to make sure they're growing well and don't need special care. Keep a special watch out for aphids and other pests.

- Water regularly to keep soil from drying out.

- Don't fertilize new roses until the first bloom period is finished.

- Refer to "Rose Care" on page 51 for information on all the basics of watering, feeding, and preventing pests and diseases so your roses continue to grow and produce beautiful, healthy blooms.

Climbing roses may need more maintenance than shrub roses because you
have to train them to grow where you
want them, but in general, pruning
roses isn't nearly as difficult as many
people imagine.

chapter five

Rose Care

Combine careful plant selection, good soil preparation, and proper planting with the organic rose care techniques described in this chapter, and you'll be rewarded with gorgeous flowers and attractive landscape plants. And best of all, the care you give to your roses will require only a few hours per season. What could be easier?

START OFF RIGHT

Many homeowners shy away from growing roses because they think that roses are too hard to care for. In fact, you may have heard that you can't grow roses without using pesticides, that pruning roses is complicated, and that roses need lots of watering.

Growing roses *can* be a lot of work—if you're growing disease-susceptible, thirsty, fertilizer-hungry cultivars in a cold climate. However, if you make careful selections (see "Choosing & Using Roses" on page 7) and plant roses that are pest- and disease-resistant and right for your climate, you'll find that growing roses is infinitely easier than you suspected. (Just keep in mind that if you've treated your rose bushes with chemicals in the past, it will take some time—at least two years—before organic methods will fully control rose pests and diseases. So be prepared to be patient!)

That's not to say that you don't have to take care of your roses once they're planted. But when you follow the maintenance basics covered in this chapter—mulching, proper pruning, organic fertilizing, and appropriate winterizing for your region—you'll be able to cut down on weeding and watering and even substantially reduce potential problems with insects and diseases.

> **If you plant roses that are pest- and disease-resistant and right for your climate, you'll find that growing roses is infinitely easier than you suspected.**

MULCHING

One of the simplest, most inexpensive things you can do to keep your roses healthy and to cut down on maintenance is to spread a layer of mulch around your rosebushes. One application of an organic mulch like shredded leaves each spring benefits your roses and other plants in so many ways.

- Reduces the need for watering
- Controls weeds
- Moderates soil temperature
- Reduces soil erosion
- Enriches soil
- Improves soil structure
- Keeps soil from splashing up onto leaves and flowers when it rains
- Improves the appearance of your garden

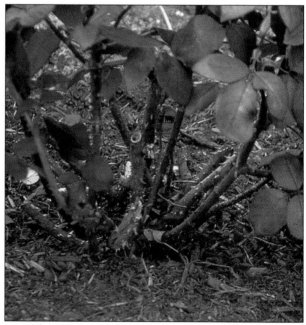

A 2-inch layer of shredded bark is an attractive mulch that will help keep your roses from drying out.

MATERIALS FOR MULCH

MULCHING WITH PLANT RESIDUES like chopped leaves or compost is one of the most important gardening techniques you can use. Not only does mulch help keep moisture in the soil, but it also can help prevent disease. Here are some of the best choices for your roses.

Cocoa hulls. The dark brown shells of cocoa beans are attractive, easy to apply, and fairly stable (they absorb $2\frac{1}{2}$ times their weight in water). Their appealing chocolate scent disappears quickly but makes them fun to apply. Cocoa hulls are sold in bags.

Compost. Not only is finished compost the best soil amendment but it's also an attractive mulch, especially if the composted materials have been shredded for an even texture. Use homemade compost, or buy it bagged.

Grass clippings. One of the most accessible and inexpensive mulches, grass clippings are also a quick source of nitrogen. But there are some drawbacks—clippings can form a thick mat that water can't penetrate. Clippings also decompose quickly, building up a great deal of damaging heat and making them short-lived as a mulch. If you use grass clippings, apply no more than a 2-inch layer.

(continued on page 54)

Leaves. For roses, leaves are best used shredded or composted into leaf mold because unshredded tree leaves tend to become a sodden mess that can prevent rain water from getting to the soil where the roots can use it. Shredded leaves, however, make an attractive mulch.

Manure. Manure must be aged for six months before it's used as a mulch so that it doesn't burn plants. An advantage of using manure for mulch is that it's rich in nutrients. It will help strengthen your roses, even if they've been growing in the same location for several years. Don't let manure come into direct contact with rose stems, however. Buy it in bulk from a farm or in bags from a garden center.

Shredded bark and wood chips. Commercially available bark may come from fir, pine, cedar, or hardwood trees. Wood chips are usually available in bulk from tree-trimming companies free of charge or for a nominal cost. One drawback is that fresh wood chips tie up soil nitrogen as they break down, making it unavailable to plants. To counteract this, spread 1 inch of compost or aged manure on the soil before adding bark or wood chips, or apply a high-nitrogen fertilizer such as bloodmeal or bonemeal.

TIPS FOR WATERING WISELY

Certain rose species and cultivars—especially rugosa roses—are very tolerant of dry conditions. Many other cultivars grow adequately with normal rainfall but really show off with just a bit of extra watering. Even when you need to supplement what Mother Nature provides, there are tricks to help your roses thrive with less water, as well as ways to conserve water.

Choose your site carefully. Don't grow roses in windy locations because exposure to wind causes both plants and soil to lose water quickly. Avoid naturally dry sites, such as under eaves and next to south-facing walls.

Prepare the soil well. Organic matter helps the soil retain moisture longer, while at the same time increasing aeration around the roots so they don't get waterlogged. When planting, enrich the soil with plenty of compost, shredded leaves, or other organic matter, and work the soil as deeply as possible to encourage deep rooting.

An inexpensive way to "install" a drip irrigation system is to lay a soaker hose beside your plants, then cover the soil and hose with mulch. When you want to water, just hook up your garden hose to the soaker hose. When you're done, disconnect the garden hose, and no one will ever know that the soaker hose is there!

Mulch. Apply a 3-inch layer of organic mulch around the base of your roses to slow down moisture loss. (See "Mulching" on page 52.)

Use drip irrigation. Drip irrigation delivers moisture directly to the soil with no runoff, so your roses get the benefit of every drop.

Stick with organic fertilizers. For plants to absorb nutrients from the soil, the soil needs to be moist. Fast-acting chemical fertilizers require large amounts of water to be effective, and the resulting lush, succulent growth is a water hog. Slower-acting organic fertilizers produce roses that need less water.

Water deeply. Deep-rooted plants have the greatest chance of surviving droughts because even at the height of summer, the soil 8 to 18 inches deep remains moist for a week or more. Encourage deep rooting by soaking the soil thoroughly at long intervals.

Water only when necessary. Don't automatically water every week—dig into the soil before watering to see if the top 3 to 4 inches is dry. If it is, turn on the tap. Otherwise, just stop and smell the roses!

FEEDING ROSES NATURALLY

Fertilizer needs vary based on your type of soil and growing conditions, but no matter where you live, your roses are going to need the essential nutrients.

The Big 3—NPK

A regular fertilizing schedule will help to keep your roses robust. Of all the plant nutrients, nitrogen (N), phosphorus (P), and potassium (K) are needed in the greatest quantities. These elements are represented in the above order in the three numbers listed on fertilizer bags and boxes.

Other nutrients are also important, including sulfur, calcium, and magnesium. Your roses also need trace elements (called micronutrients) in smaller quantities.

quick tip

Always water your roses the day before feeding and again after applying fertilizer. This helps prevent fertilizer burn.

Nitrogen. Plants need more nitrogen than any other nutrient. With adequate nitrogen, plants have strong, sturdy growth with lots of leaves and flowers. Nitrogen leaches rapidly from the soil and plants quickly use it, so you'll have to supply it throughout the growing season.

Phosphorus. Phosphorus is found in much smaller amounts than nitrogen in plants, but it's essential for root growth. Phosphorus also helps plant tissues to mature, which is critical for winter hardiness.

Potassium. Potassium helps plant foods move throughout the plant, and without it, roses will have poor flower production. If your garden soil is sandy, you'll need to apply potassium fertilizers more often.

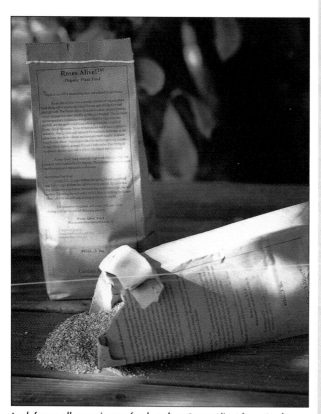

Look for an all-organic rose food, such as Roses Alive! from Gardens Alive! It will provide a well-balanced diet for any type of rose.

CLUES TO NUTRIENT NEEDS

IT'S BEST TO feed your roses on a regular schedule, but even then, your plants may require more or less of a specific type of fertilizer. If your plants are looking less than perfect, figure out what they're hungry for by checking for the following clues.

- Stunted growth with pale green or yellow leaves, weak stems—nitrogen deficiency

- Lots of leaves, but few flowers and poor root development—too much nitrogen

- Dark green leaves on top; red to purple on the undersides—potassium deficiency

- Weak stems, low disease resistance, wilting, and poor flower production—potassium deficiency

Fertilizing Dos and Don'ts

● Do fertilize about two weeks after spring pruning. Roses benefit from annual springtime applications of complete organic fertilizers.

● Do apply fertilizer after the heavy blooming period in early summer to encourage reblooming.

● Do fertilize again after the second bloom cycle. (If you live in Zone 9 or 10, you can fertilize twice after the second bloom cycle, four to six weeks apart.)

● Don't add nitrogen-rich fertilizers within six weeks of the first frost date in your area. Late feedings encourage tender green growth, which frost will kill.

● Don't feed newly planted roses until they have completed their first bloom cycle.

● Don't use as much fertilizer for miniature roses as is recommended for other roses.

Organic Fertilizers for Roses

Fertilizer Type	Percentage of Nutrients	Comments
Alfalfa meal	5% nitrogen; 1% phosphorus; 2% potassium	One of the most recommended fertilizers for roses
Bloodmeal	10%–15% nitrogen	Fast-acting nitrogen source
Bonemeal	34% phosphorus	Good source of phosphorus; raises pH
Compost	0.5%–4% nitrogen, phosphorus, and potassium	Slow-acting fertilizer; excellent soil conditioner
Fish emulsion	4%–5% nitrogen; 1%–4% phosphorus; 1%–2% potassium; 5% sulfur	Can be applied as a foliar spray to revitalize leaves
Greensand	1% phosphorus, 6%–7% potassium	Slow release of nutrients and trace minerals
Manure	2%–4% nitrogen; 1%–2% phosphorus and potassium	Use composted or dehydrated manure that is aged rather than fresh.

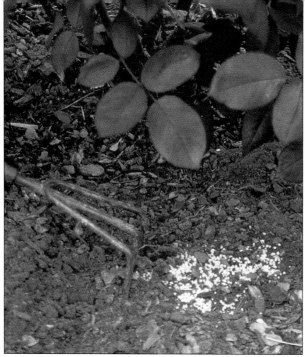

Scratch fertilizer into the soil around your roses and water well to help the soil absorb it.

ROSE PRUNING BASICS

You may be nervous about pruning your roses, but don't worry—even if you make a wrong cut or two, roses are very forgiving. Roses are naturally self-renewing, producing strong new shoots from the base of the plant each year, giving you a new chance for beautiful blossoms—and another try at pruning.

When to Prune

For most roses, the time to do major pruning is later winter or early spring, or about four to six weeks before the last killing frost in your area. By then most winterkill will have occurred but new growth won't have started.

Summer pruning is really just a matter of removing the faded flowers throughout the growing season. Because this promotes new growth, stop pruning in late summer so that there won't be soft new growth that will be prone to winter damage.

MORE ROSE PRUNING TIPS

PRUNING ROSES doesn't have to be scary—or painful. These tips will help you make quick and easy work of the job.

- Wear a long-sleeve shirt or jacket, pants, and leather or plastic- or rubber-coated gloves for protection when you prune. Roses are thorny!

- Keep pruning shears, lopping shears, and your saw sharpened so that cuts are clean and stems aren't crushed.

- Dispose of rose clippings by burning them or sealing them in plastic trash bags for disposal with your household trash. Don't compost them because they can be a breeding ground for insects and diseases.

To give a nice shape to your roses and help improve air circulation, prune side shoots that are growing inward or crossing with other canes.

What to Prune

The toughest decision in pruning roses is deciding what to leave alone and what to cut off. But if you follow the commonsense pruning rules below, you'll wonder why you ever worried about pruning your roses. Most vigorous-growing roses can be pruned back to 6 inches tall, while others can be pruned to 10 to 12 inches without harm.

For all roses. Remove suckers, dead and diseased canes, canes that don't flower well, canes that are crossed and rubbing others, and canes that are growing inward. If roses are grafted onto rootstock, suckers may emerge from the stem just below the ground. Remove these shoots so they don't crowd out the grafted cultivar. Don't just cut them off at the ground, or they will resprout. Use a trowel to follow the shoot underground to where it joins the understock, and snap the shoot off with the trowel.

For hybrid tea roses.
Cut the oldest stems off at the base, leaving three to six healthy canes; prune the remaining canes to shape the plant.

For floribunda roses.
Remove the oldest stems at the base, leaving six to eight healthy canes; prune off the top third of each remaining cane.

For climbers. Prune climbers to train and shape them, cutting back side branches to about 6 inches; leave more canes than on other roses—about 15 or so—to get a good flush of bloom next year.

For ramblers. Ramblers are pruned more heavily because they bloom on first-year wood; prune back to 12 to 18 inches from the ground each year.

For shrub roses. Prune off the top third of new canes, and cut side shoots on older growth to 4 to 6 inches.

How to Prune

Now that you know *when* to prune and *what* to prune, you need to know *how* to prune.

- Make cuts ¼ inch above an outward-facing bud—the point where a leaf is or was attached to the stem.
- Cut at a 45-degree angle away from the bud. Growth from an outward-

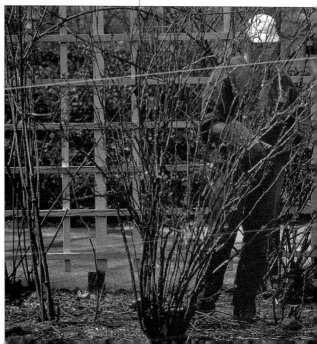

Prune hybrid tea roses in early spring by cutting away all but the healthiest canes at the base of the plant (above). Leave three to six canes for a new season of growth.

Shrub roses aren't cut back as dramatically (below), but you will need to cut back side shoots to produce a new season of blooms.

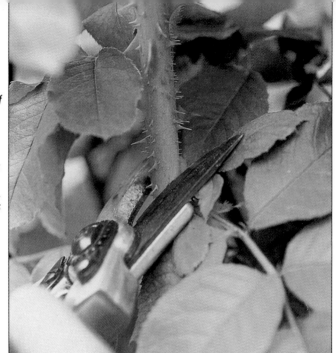

When pruning any rose, make cuts at a 45-degree angle so water will run off the cut surface (to reduce the risk of disease infection). Also be sure to cut back to a five-leaflet node. Three-leaflet leaves appear on the younger, thinner parts of the canes, and if new growth sprouts from these areas, it will be too weak to support blooms.

facing bud promotes open growth in the center of the bush, encouraging air to circulate, preventing disease from developing, and allowing light to reach into the plant for better growth. Angling the cut so it slopes away from the bud prevents moisture from gathering in the bud and rotting it.

- Cut back to at least a five-leaflet node. Otherwise, the sprouting stem will be weak and spindly.
- If the inside, or pith, of the cane is discolored, then cut the shoot back until the pith is white and healthy.
- If, after pruning, two or three shoots emerge from one eye, or bud, pinch out all but one.

WINTER CARE FOR YOUR ROSES

For northern gardeners, having roses that survive the winter with flying colors depends on a number of factors, including the natural hardiness of the rose cultivar, how well you've hardened off the plants in the fall, and the severity of the winter cold and winds.

Of course, you can't control the weather conditions, but you can take steps to protect your roses from harsh winter weather.

Winter Hardiness

It's easiest for you and best for your plants if you grow roses that are hardy in your climate and don't need extra winter protection. When buying roses, look for ones that are hardy in your zone (see the USDA Plant Hardiness Zones map on page 106 if you're unsure which zone you live in). But if you're determined to grow rose cultivars that are slightly tender, increase their chances of survival with pegging or caging.

Pegging

Pegging is the preferred winter-protection technique for tender climbing roses. Just bend the canes to the ground and peg them in place with stakes or wire, then cover them with a foot of soil, leaves, or straw. Remove pegs in spring. To learn how to make stakes or wire staples for pegging roses, turn to page 34.

Trenching

The easiest way to protect standard or tree roses from chilling winter winds is to keep them potted and move them into the garage for the winter. If you prefer to have them growing in the garden, then trenching is the best technique to help these tall roses survive northern winters.

After pruning the rose, remove the stake and loosen the soil around the plant's root with a shovel. Dig a trench about 8 inches deep and long enough to fit the plant in. Slowly topple the rose into the trench holding it by the middle of the trunk. Fill the trench with soil, mounding it over the plant. Add 1 foot or more of mulch—leaves and straw are best—on top for extra protection.

quick tip

If you live in Zone 9 or 10, protecting your roses from harsh winter winds and deep freezes isn't much of a concern. However, you can still provide winter care for your roses, namely keeping fungal diseases in check because the temperature won't get cold enough to kill them.

If your roses showed any signs of black spot, make sure you strip any infected leaves from your plants, and prune off infected canes. Also clean up any fallen leaves around the base of your plants because black spot will overwinter there. Destroy all infected materials; don't compost them because it's unlikely that the compost will get hot enough to kill the spores.

Hybrid tea roses aren't cold-hardy, and their canes aren't flexible enough to be pegged to the ground for protection. Caging them is a good way to keep these tender plants warm for the winter. A chicken-wire cylinder filled with shredded leaves or straw will protect the bud union from freezing.

Caging

Mound 1 foot of soil over the base of the plant for insulation. Then make a wire-mesh cylinder around the plant, or use a tomato cage. Mound soil around the outside of the cylinder base to stabilize it. Fill the cylinder with a lightweight mulch of leaves or straw. In the spring, remove the cylinder and mulch, and gently wash off the extra soil.

Hardening Off

New growth is most susceptible to winter damage, so harden off your roses (give them time for all stems to become woody) before frost hits. To harden off roses, stop pruning and fertilizing with nitrogen four to six weeks before the first fall frost. Also, gradually reduce watering during this time period.

TAKING CONTROL OF PESTS AND DISEASES

The easiest and most efficient way to beat rose problems is to keep them from happening in the first place. A preventive approach is key: Choose resistant cultivars, keep your plants healthy by giving them the right growing conditions, and practice strategic pruning and good garden hygiene. Your plants will stand a better chance against pests and diseases if they're growing well when the problems arise.

Good Practices Prevent Diseases

- Choose pest- and disease-resistant plants.

- Watch how you water. Black spot and rust spores must be in water to germinate, so it's important to keep rose foliage as dry as possible if these diseases are a problem in your area.

- Space plants properly (see page 46 for guidelines). Plant roses in a sunny site, and prune them to create open centers—and you'll keep moisture-loving diseases such as powdery mildew and black spot at bay.

- Keep the garden clean. Remove and destroy damaged leaves, stems, and flowers as they appear. Burn them, bury them 3 feet deep, or send them to a landfill. Don't compost them because you can end up spreading diseases all over your garden.

- Mulch for disease control. Mulching prevents overwintering disease spores on the ground from reaching your plants. After removing all fallen leaves in the fall, apply several inches of mulch. Put down a fresh layer after the late winter or early spring pruning.

- Don't overfertilize. Too much nitrogen fertilizer can lead to too much leaf growth (and fewer flowers)—which is just what aphids are looking for.

SUDS WASH AWAY PESTS AND DISEASES

YOU CAN MAKE a spray from soap and water that will kill most soft-bodied insects such as aphids, thrips, and mites. It's easy to do, and insecticidal soaps are nontoxic to people, birds, or other animals.

Use 1 to 3 teaspoons of mild household soap, such as Ivory Snow, per 1 gallon of water. Or try commercial insecticidal soaps like Safer Insecticidal Soap or Aphid-Mite Attack, applied according to the manufacturer's recommendations.

Soaps may be ineffective with hard water. If a scum and milky-looking curds form, use bottled water to make your soap solution.

To control fungal diseases like powdery mildew, mix a simple solution of 1 tablespoon baking soda and 1 gallon of water to spray on roses. If you've had trouble with fungal diseases in the past, start spraying roses on a weekly basis *before* disease symptoms start.

ROSE PROBLEMS AND ORGANIC CONTROLS

Even with careful rose selection, proper growing conditions, and the right doses of organic fertilizers, roses can sometimes still be bothered by pests or diseases. Use this at-a-glance information to find out what's bugging your roses and what to do about it.

BLACK SPOT

Black-spot spores must be in water to germinate, so careful watering is the easiest way to prevent this unsightly disease.

Symptoms: Black spot first appears as black or brown spots on leaves at the bottom of the plant. The spots may blend to form blotches on leaves and canes. In severe cases, entire leaves will turn yellow and eventually fall off.

Solutions: Avoid wetting rose leaves when watering, and mulch the bed to keep spores from bouncing up on plants when it rains. Remove crowded canes (to improve air circulation), the lowest leaves from the base of each plant, and any infected foliage. Spray infected plants with garden sulfur.

MOSAIC VIRUS

While mosaic virus damage may not look as devastating as that of other rose diseases, there's no remedy for the virus. If these symptoms show up on one of your rosebushes, you'll have to destroy it.

Symptoms: A number of viral diseases may attack roses. Mosaic virus is a common type. Leaves develop yellow-green mottling or odd patterns that bear no resemblance to chewing or sucking damage. Leaves may also develop yellow netting. The foliage may curl and growth may be stunted.

Solutions: There's no cure for viral diseases. Destroy infected plants immediately. Insects like aphids can spread viruses from plant to plant as they feed, so controlling the insects is a way to help prevent the spread of this disease.

POWDERY MILDEW

Symptoms: Powdery mildew is a fungal disease that starts on young growth as raised blisters and causes leaves to curl. Eventually new leaves and flower buds are coated with a thin, white, powdery substance and growth becomes deformed. Older growth is usually not affected.

Powdery mildew spores germinate best in dry conditions. If it's a problem in your area, control it early by washing the leaves or spraying them with compost tea.

Solutions: Remove crowded canes and infected leaves. Control powdery mildew with weekly sprays of 1 tablespoon of baking soda mixed with 1 gallon of water, or with compost tea. (Steep 1 gallon of compost in 5 gallons of water for three days; strain.)

RUST

Symptoms: Rust is another fungal disease that can attack roses, but it is most common on the West Coast. It appears in spring as small orange spots on the undersides of lower leaves and as light yellow spots on the upper sides. Long, narrow spots may appear on the canes. In summer, masses of spores form on the undersides of leaves, and upper surfaces will have dead spots surrounded by green or red. In fall, black spores appear in these spots. Leaves may drop off in summer or fall.

Rust is most common on the West Coast, and like black spot, its spores must be in water to germinate.

Solutions: Start checking foliage in early spring and cut off diseased leaves. When conditions are cool and damp, spray weekly with fungicidal soap. Otherwise, avoid wetting rose leaves when watering, and mulch the bed to keep spores from bouncing up on plants when it rains. Remove crowded canes (to improve air circulation), the lowest leaves from the base of each plant, and any infected foliage.

Aphids are wingless in most stages of their life, so you can knock them off your rosebuds and foliage with a spray of water. The force of the water will kill most of them, and the others won't be able to return.

Symptoms: These soft-bodied, ⅛-inch-long sucking insects can be red, green, pink, brown, or black. They're most common in early spring on soft new growth, clustering on tips of young leaves and stems, flower buds, and blooms. Foliage and flowers may be dwarfed or disfigured. The honeydew-like substance excreted by aphids attracts ants and may develop sooty mold.

Solutions: Prune off heavily infested parts of the rose and destroy them. Use less nitrogen fertilizer (so your roses don't over-produce new growth that attracts aphids). Dislodge aphids with a strong spray of water or use insecticidal soap. Encourage beneficial insects, such as lady beetles, to inhabit your garden with mixed plantings.

Copper-colored, green-headed Japanese beetles skeletonize leaves and chew holes in flowers and buds. Other types of beetles cause the same types of damage.

◀--- **BEETLES** --

Symptoms: White grubs, the larvae of Japanese beetles, spend winter in the soil. In spring, they emerge as adult Japanese beetles that chew on roses in gardens east of the Mississippi. Japanese beetles aren't the only type of beetles to attack roses, however—they're just ones that most folks are familiar with. Roses can also be bothered by spotted cucumber beetles, fuller rose beetles, goldsmith beetles, June beetles, and rose chafers.

Solutions: Whatever type of beetle your roses may attract, the solutions are the same. Apply milky spore disease to your lawn to help control grubs in the soil; follow package directions. Use Japanese beetle traps, placed 50 feet downwind from roses, or pick beetles off by hand and drop them in soapy water.

CANE BORERS

Symptoms: Larvae of various insects enter stems and canes from cut ends, causing shoots to wilt, be stunted, or die back. Damage is mainly cosmetic.

- *Small carpenter bees:* ½-inch-long blue-green bees most often lay eggs in canes with cut ends; larvae bore out the soft center of the stems.

- *Rose stem girdlers:* Larvae spiral around inside canes, causing stems to swell and split; green-bronze beetles appear in summer.

- *Rose stem sawflies:* Wasplike insects with clear wings appear in summer; larvae bore into canes causing wilt and dieback.

Solutions: Prune off the canes below the infested part and destroy them. To prevent borers from entering canes, paint pruning cuts with wood glue, shellac, or nail polish.

Wormlike larvae of carpenter bees, rose stem girdlers, or rose stem sawflies bore holes in canes, causing growth above the hole to wilt.

SPIDER MITES

Symptoms: Microscopic red, brown, yellow, or green sucking mites that cause leaves to be stippled with yellow, red, or gray. Leaves will curl up and fall off. Webbing may appear on undersides of leaves. Spider mites are worst in hot, dry weather.

Solutions: Mites overwinter on weeds and garden trash, so clean up the garden well in fall and early spring. Destroy overwintering eggs with dormant oil spray in late winter. In hot, dry weather, wash foliage once or twice a week. If infestation is apparant, wash foliage three days in a row. Spray heavy infestations with insecticidal soap every three to five days for a two-week period.

Prevent severe infestations of spider mites by cleaning up garden debris in the fall so they won't have a spot to overwinter.

'Climbing Cécile Brunner' roses seem right at home climbing on this Victorian house surrounded by a cottage garden. Even if you don't have an English-style house, there are many ways you can use roses—climbing and otherwise—to dress up your landscape.

chapter six

Landscaping with Roses

Roses are perfect landscape plants because you can use them in so many ways. Think of them as part shrub, part perennial, and part vine. Some varieties offer season-long blooms, and many produce brightly colored hips that add a burst of color to your landscape throughout the fall and winter, too.

USE ROSES ANYWHERE

Roses are great planted with herbs, in a cottage garden, or in a perennial flowerbed. You can also use roses as hedges or train them to climb arbors, trellises, walls, even lampposts. Your imagination is the only limit to creating a beautiful and interesting garden with roses.

A GALLERY OF IDEAS

Once you've summed up the all the ways you can use roses in your landscape, it's time to review the possibilities in more detail. If you need more information about specific roses, refer back to "Choosing & Using Roses" on page 7. The information contained there, combined with the gallery of photos in this chapter, will help you decide exactly how and where you should use roses on your property and which roses are the best choices for your intended use.

In this chapter, you'll find ideas for different types of plantings from low-growing groundcovers to 20-foot climbers. You'll also find tips to help you train climbers and ramblers, as well as suggestions for what to plant with roses to show them off to their best advantage.

Your imagination is the only limit to creating a beautiful and interesting garden with roses.

What better way to lead visitors through your rose garden than an arbor covered in beautiful blooms. 'Royal Sunset' flanks the left side of the arbor while 'Handel' adorns the other side.

THE ROSE GARDEN

The time-honored way to use roses in the landscape is to plant a rose garden—with roses in the spotlight and no supporting players. If your heart is set on a rose garden, by all means plant one, but don't grow the roses all by themselves. A bed with nothing in it but roses will attract pests and diseases, and it will look dull when the roses have finished blooming.

● Underplant your roses with herbs like lavender and catmint (*Nepeta* × *faassenii*) for a lovely contrast.

● Choose a mixture of repeat-blooming roses, including hybrid teas, floribundas, grandifloras, miniatures, shrubs, rugosas, polyanthas, and repeat-blooming old roses for a garden that will be full of blooms throughout the season.

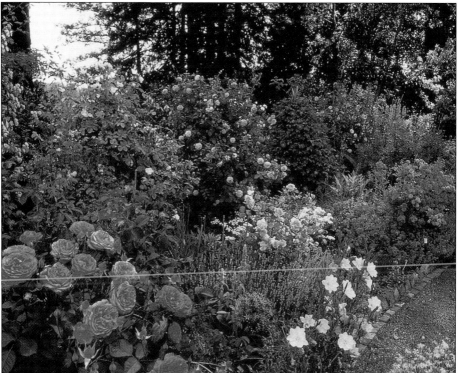

Polyantha 'Ballerina' is nestled behind an informal planting of white gaura, violas, and other perennials (top), while a variety of climbing, shrub, and polyantha roses form a backdrop for catmint, lamb's-ears, star of Persia, and pasqueflower (bottom).

PERENNIAL AND SHRUB BORDERS

Roses are natural partners in the perennial garden, adding height, texture, fragrance, and even season-long bloom. Shrub, old garden, species, and grandiflora roses are all excellent choices for a perennial border.

Plant tall roses in the back of the bed, shorter ones in the middle, and minis in the front, the same way you'd use perennials. In an island bed designed to be seen from all sides, put the tallest plants in the center and work down from there.

In mixed shrub borders, where roses share the billing with other plants, multiseasonal interest isn't critical for each rose—other plants can easily take over when rose bloom is past. In both perennial and shrub borders, you can base your choice of roses on color, plant and flower form, and personal preference.

Roses provide background interest in this mixed border and also share the foreground spotlight with May night salvia, pinks, and yarrow.

Catmint bows gracefully in front of shrub roses at the corner of this deckside herb and flower garden.

ROSES WITH HERBS

No type of garden is more romantic or has as much historical significance than an herb garden. People have used herbs as medicines, cosmetics, seasonings for foods, and decorations throughout the ages. For many centuries, roses were an integral part of herb gardens, so selecting an old rose or two to compliment your herb garden is a wonderful choice. 'Apothecary's Rose' (*Rosa gallica* var. *officinalis*) is probably the rose grown in western gardens the longest. It has magenta, semidouble flowers that bloom in early summer—a perfect partner for lavender- and white-blooming herbs.

Don't be afraid to use culinary herbs as well as more decorative herbs to hide the base of leggy rose canes. Sweet basil, curly parsley, chives, French tarragon, 'Fernleaf' dill, and others are not only pretty to look at but are useful, too.

WHAT TO PLANT WITH ROSES

WOULDN'T IT be easy if there were simply a list of plants to choose from? What you plant with roses depends on what you like, what color roses you're planting, and what your planting conditions are. Here are some ideas to get you started.

- Ornamental grasses add a graceful linear quality to the garden.

- Blue-flowering perennials complement the warm shades of red, pink, magenta, yellow, and peach.

- White-flowering perennials open up the garden and show up beautifully even when it's dark outside (so they're a great choice if you like to sit out in your garden in the evening).

- Plants that repeat the bloom colors of your roses are a good choice because the colors won't clash.

- Low-growing plants—either flowering or strictly foliage— that cover the bare lower parts of the rose canes create a nice two-tier effect.

ROSES ON STRUCTURES

You may want to dress up or hide a fence, arbor, trellis, pergola, wall, building, or other structure with roses. The tall climbers, ramblers, and more aggressive shrub and old roses are ideal for this purpose. Use the shorter climbers for low fences or train them on pillars.

Miniature climbers have a powerful impact for their diminutive size. An ideal place for a miniature climber is on a mailbox or lamppost.

Combine roses with other climbers like clematis for even more beauty and bloom. Underplant with cheerful annuals in complementary colors or with cool foliage plants like hostas to create ground-level interest.

With a little guidance from you, your climbers and ramblers will create a stunning landscaping effect. Use

The luscious apricot, fully double blooms of 'Alchymist' roses soften the look of this informal split-rail fence and make a perfect choice for a natural-looking landscape.

raffia or rubber- or plastic-coated wire for the ties, making a figure-eight between the cane and the support so the tie won't put pressure on the cane.

Training Roses to a Fence

Ramblers are the best type of rose to train to a fence. Train the canes to grow horizontally on the fence for best bloom. When the main canes are forced to grow horizontally, they will produce more new shoots that will bear the blooms. As canes die or stop flowering well, untie them and cut them off at the base because ramblers bloom only on new wood.

Training Roses to a Trellis

Train climbing roses to a trellis by starting on the outside of the plant and working across, spacing the canes evenly against the trellis as you tie them to it. The more horizontally you bend and tie the canes, the more flowers you'll have. Train climbers to an arbor in the same way, planting a rose on each side of the arbor.

What could be more inviting than an entryway covered in fragrant blooms? Here, red-orange 'Delber's Orange Climber' and white 'Lace Cascade' invite all who pass by to stop and smell the roses.

ROSES AS GROUNDCOVERS

quick tip

You can cover a slope with climbing roses, too, if you choose a flexible-caned variety such as 'Madame Plantier' that will fill out a 6- to 8-foot area. As the branches of the rose lengthen, peg them to the ground with wire pins, as described on page 34.

Planting low-growing, sprawling roses is an excellent solution for hard-to-mow slopes, as long as the slope isn't too dry. Although the foliage of groundcover roses isn't as dense as that of traditional groundcovers such as pachysandra, it's thick enough to serve the purpose. *Rosa wichuraiana,* climbing roses like 'New Dawn', and some of the Meidiland landscape rose cultivars such as 'Alba Meidiland' make colorful, effective groundcovers. They're most effective if you install them with a combination of plastic mulch and an organic mulch like bark chips, or with a thick organic mulch like shredded leaves.

Other excellent choices for groundcover roses include the following:

The 'Mme. Issac Pereire' rose in the foreground is actually a shrub rose, but its 6-foot-long canes were pegged to the ground to cascade over the stone wall.

- 'Sea Foam', a repeat-blooming creamy white rose that grows 2 feet tall × 8 feet wide

- 'The Fairy', a repeat-blooming double pink polyantha rose that grows 2 feet tall × 3 feet wide

- Miniature roses, such as 'Snow Carpet', which grows 1 foot tall × 3 feet wide

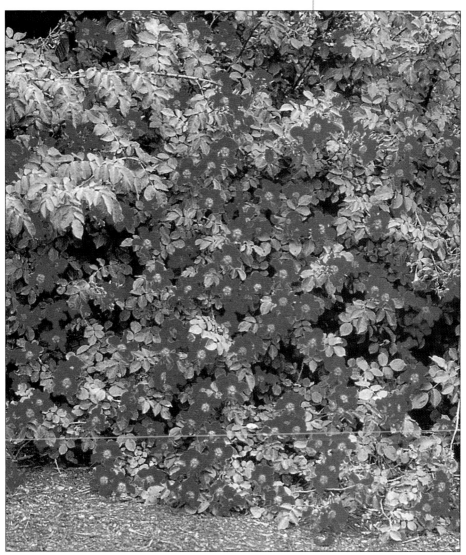

Groundcovers don't have to fade into the lawn. You can make a bold statement with 'Red Max Graf', a frost-resistant groundcover rose with ruffled-edge red petals and tiny white centers.

'Complicata' roses form a low hedge as they grow along the inside of a traditional picket fence. They make a beautiful screen and sound barrier to the street on the other side of the fence.

ROSE HEDGES AND EDGINGS

Shrub, old garden, and taller grandiflora roses are perfect for creating hedges as a background, screen, or barrier. Although the plants lose their leaves in winter, the thorny branches still serve as a physical barrier and also provide shelter for wildlife. Many of these roses have beautiful hips in fall and winter, so they add color to the winter landscape and attract birds to your yard. You can mix roses of similar size and compatible flower colors, or mix roses with other shrubs for a more informal, colorful hedge.

To create a thick, blooming tall hedge, you simply have to pick the right rose—one that's upright, densely bushy, and disease-resistant so it doesn't need coddling. See "Choosing & Using Roses" on page 7 for suggestions.

If you'd like a low hedge or edging, there are plenty of options. Instead of a sprawling groundcover rose, choose one that's more upright but only reaches a mature height of 1 to 4 feet tall. Most floribundas, polyanthas, and miniature roses grow beautifully as low hedges, which are useful along walks and paths and around terraces and beds. They make a clear boundary but don't block the view.

A tall rose hedge makes a pretty screen to block out unsightly views. When blooms are finished, bluebirds and mockingbirds will feed on the hips and other songbirds will use the thicket for shelter and nesting.

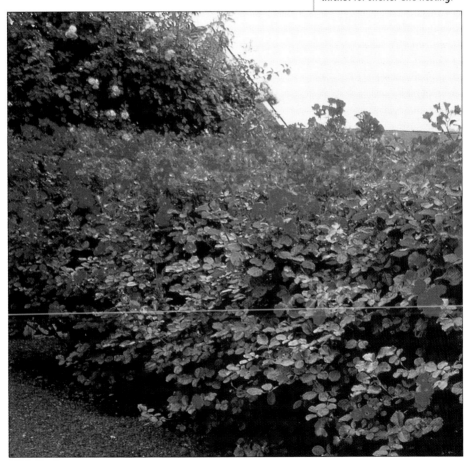

CHOOSING THE RIGHT CONTAINER

JUST ABOUT ANY PLANT can be grown in a container. The container size should be in proportion to the plant's natural garden size, although particularly large plants will never attain the same size as they would in the ground.

For most full-size roses, the minimum pot size is 14 inches deep and 18 inches wide. Miniatures need pots 6 to 10 inches in diameter. You can use any substantial vessel that can hold potting soil. A wide range of pots are available at garden centers. You can even hide an ugly plastic pot in an attractive cachepot or plastic-lined basket.

ROSES IN CONTAINERS

One of the greatest pleasures of container gardening is that it's like having furniture. You can move the containers around to suit your mood or the occasion. The best arrangements of containers are in informally arranged, odd-numbered groups of different-size pots, but it's always fun to experiment with different looks and groupings.

Roses look lovely in containers. The miniature roses and shorter-sprawling cultivars are graceful in hanging baskets. You can also grow roses in containers to place on decks, terraces, porches, and patios and throughout the yard.

Smaller-growing types such as miniature roses are perfect choices for containers, as are the floribundas and polyanthas. Combine roses with annuals like ivy geraniums, annual candytuft, sweet alyssum,

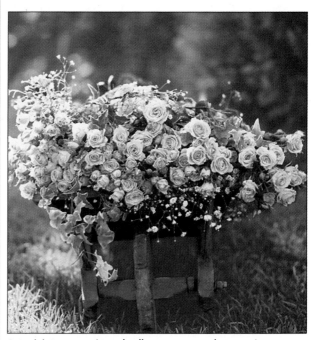

Put miniature roses in a wheelbarrow or any other container, and you can move them wherever you want a splash of color in your garden.

These 'Mister Lincoln' standard roses create a formal and fragrant entryway. If you live where winters are harsh, plant them in pots so they can overwinter away from strong winds and freezing temperatures.

and petunias for two-story color. Or create a more subtle look with herbs like prostrate rosemary or creeping thyme.

Overwintering potted roses in colder climates requires some effort, so be prepared to bring them indoors or provide protection if you live where temperatures dip below 20°F. Standard, or tree, roses are also perfect for container growing. Standard roses have a tough time surviving in winter winds, so it's best to bring them inside during the winter. When you grow a standard rose in a container, it's easy to move it in and out of your house.

quick tip

Before you set potted roses back outside in early spring, take them out of their containers, cut through crossing or circling roots to prevent girdling, and replant them with new potting soil. Like any other container-grown plant, soil nutrients are used up and washed away with each watering, so don't forget to feed them.

One of the joys of rose gardening is being able to bring the beauty and fragrance of roses indoors, even if the arrangement is as simple as this cluster of 'Color Magic' hybrid tea roses.

chapter seven

Roses as Cut Flowers

There's nothing more elegant than a bouquet of roses, and when you grow your own, you can bring in armfuls of roses from the garden to enjoy without spending a fortune at a flower shop!

MAKE THE MOST OF YOUR ROSES

In this chapter, you'll learn how to cut and condition your roses properly so they have the longest vase life possible—nine days or more. You'll also learn how to show off your cut roses to their best advantage. You could just stick a bunch of roses in a jelly jar. But, if you arrange them in that jelly jar, you can let your creative juices produce a display that does justice to your beautiful blossoms.

Luckily, casual, simple arrangements are the style today, rather than the more stiff, formal, rule-bound arrangements of the past. Even so, to create the most satisfying arrangements, you will need to pay attention to a few guidelines regarding size, balance, color, and shape. With a little practice, you'll be able to fashion beautiful arrangements and savor the fruits of your gardening labors. But first, let's take a look at how to cut roses properly.

WHEN AND HOW TO CUT ROSES

To enjoy your rose arrangements the longest, cut roses from your garden either in the evening or early in the morning. This is when the plants are most filled with water. Gather rosebuds and half-open flowers, but avoid fully open roses because they won't last long. Be sure to use pruning shears, not scissors, to cut roses because scissors don't have enough leverage to cut cleanly through the woody stems.

You won't need a lot of specialized equipment to get started or to keep your roses growing in tip-top shape.

When cutting roses to bring indoors, remember to cut them at a 45-degree angle, just as you do when pruning. The angled cut will help keep your rose canes healthier.

4 Steps to Simply Beautiful Cut Roses

1. Cut stems just above a five-leaflet leaf at a 45-degree angle. It's best if the leaf is facing outward because another shoot will grow from this point. Also, consider the shape and size of the bush before cutting any roses so that you don't ruin its form.

2. Once you've cut a rose, strip the foliage from the bottom 3 to 4 inches of its stem. Carry a bucket of water with you and plunge the stems into the bucket as soon as you've cut them.

3. Once you're back indoors, recut each stem underwater at a sharp angle so that the maximum area of the cut end is exposed to water. Cut off the thorns in the area where you have stripped the foliage away, using thornstrippers or a sharp knife.

4. Set the container of roses in a dark, cool, humid place (such as a refrigerator or a basement) for at least several hours, preferably overnight, in order to condition the roses before using them in an arrangement. (Cut other flowers and foliage for your arrangement at the same time as you cut your roses and put them in that same dark, humid place as your roses to condition them, too.)

Inexpensive thornstrippers make quick work of removing prickly thorns, which in turn makes arranging roses so much easier.

MAKING CUT ROSES LAST

YOU CAN PROLONG the life of cut roses by changing the water daily and by using a floral conditioner. Floral conditioners improve water uptake and inhibit bacterial growth in cut roses by decreasing the pH of the water. You can purchase a commercial floral conditioning product or try a few household ingredients you probably already have on hand. (If your tap water is extremely alkaline or you have a water softener, use distilled water for the conditioning solution.)

- **Bleach.** Household liquid bleach can inhibit bacterial growth for several days. Mix ¼ teaspoon of bleach and 1 gallon of water.

- **Sugar.** Granulated sugar keeps the cut ends of flowers from sealing, so the buds continue to get nourishment and develop normally. Add 1 tablespoon of granulated sugar to 1 gallon of water. Use with an antibacterial agent, such as bleach.

- **Tonic water or soda.** Tonic water and citrus-flavored soda both increase acidity and supply sugar. Use 1 part soda or tonic water and 2 parts water.

- **Listerine.** Listerine or a generic substitute has antibacterial action and a trace of nutrient value. Mix 2 tablespoons of Listerine and 1 gallon of distilled water. Change the solution every three to five days.

quick tip

When considering the colors you'll be using, don't forget about green. The green of stems and foliage can help draw an arrangement together, especially if it's made with flowers of many different colors.

The medium pink English roses take center stage in this arrangement but are supported nicely by lipstick pink autumn salvia and lavender-blue larkspur.

CHOOSING COLORS

Although you don't need to know a thing about color theory to arrange a beautiful bouquet, you'll have a higher success rate if you know some elementary color combinations.

● Pairings of complementary colors such as orange and blue, yellow and purple, and red and green tend to be bright and vibrant. One example is a simple arrangement of yellow roses with purple catmint (*Nepeta* × *faassenii*).

● Related colors—such as pinks, magentas, lavenders, and purples—can also make for lovely arrangements. Imagine an arrangement of pink roses, pale pink lilies, and purple lavender.

● A monochromatic arrangement is built basically around one color. For example, a bouquet of all white to creamy white flowers, such as white roses with white larkspur (*Consolida ambigua*) and white coral bells (*Heuchera sanguinea*) accented with herb foliage would be wonderful.

● A polychromatic arrangement includes a mix of many different colors. Go to your garden, gather roses and any other flowers and foliage that catch your eye, and enjoy a bounty of beauty.

CREATING YOUR ARRANGEMENT

Styles in flower arranging are very personal, ranging from bouquets that look as though they've just been gathered from the garden to more formally arranged styles. Follow the basic principles of balance, rhythm, and scale to help guide you in making arrangements you'll love.

Balance

A balanced arrangement seems secure and stable. Balance your arrangement by putting the heavier-looking flowers toward the center and lower parts of your arrangements.

Rhythm

Rhythm is how your eyes are led from the focal point (the central point of interest) throughout the arrangement. Get rhythm in your arrangements by repeating shapes and colors and by arranging branches and stems to create a continuous flow of line.

Scale

Scale is the size relationship of the various elements. An arrangement with good scale means that the proportions of each element are pleasing and in harmony with the others. A basic guideline is that your arrangement should be 1½ times as high or as wide as the container.

quick tip

When you use floral foam to create your arrangement, be sure to soak it thoroughly under water before placing it in your container for long-lasting roses.

Notice how the large, heavy 'Sunset Celebration' roses form the center of the arrangement, while the graceful spikes of cat-mint surround them, creating balance in this casual bouquet.

All shades of roses bunched together in a galvanized watering can and a bucket create an informal yet memorable welcome to visitors.

Container Criteria

Containers can vary with the style or arrangement and type of roses. A hybrid tea rose with its long, stiff stem will work in a tall vase, while old-fashioned roses with multiple flowers on short stems lend themselves to small, informal, charming containers, such as a pottery bowl. The major point to keep in mind is that the container should complement the flowers, not detract from them. Containers that work best are those with the simplest designs or colors.

LIVE ROSE ARRANGEMENTS

For the simplest rose arrangements of all, grow miniature roses as houseplants and when they are at their peak bloom, put them in a decorative container and use them as centerpieces or room accents.

For miniatures to grow successfully indoors, they need at least 5 hours of bright sunlight in a south- or west-facing window. Or put them under fluorescent lights for 14 hours daily. Place the lights 3 to 4 inches above the tops of the plants.

Another important factor in indoor rose growing is soil moisture. Keep the soil evenly moist but not soggy. Feed your roses twice a month with a water-soluble organic fertilizer for indoor use. Miniature roses will bloom best at daytime temperatures of 70° to 75°F and nighttime temperatures of 60° to 65°F.

Growing a potted miniature rose indoors gives you an instant living arrangement that can be used as a dining room centerpiece or as a colorful accent in any room.

AIR-DRYING ROSES

DRIED ROSES have their own particular charm and are a choice pick for creating exquisite bouquets, wreaths, potpourri, and other projects. Air drying is the easiest and cheapest way to dry roses. (It works best with hybrid teas or other roses that have just one or two blooms per stem.)

Gather four to six single-stemmed roses, removing all thorns and any leaves near the base. Make sure there's no surface moisture, such as rain or dew, on the roses. Stagger the stems so that each blossom has space around it, then wrap a rubber band once or twice around the bundle of stems. Run one end of the rubber band through the other and pull up snugly. Hang the roses upside down in a warm, dark, dry, well-ventilated place. The roses are dry when the stems snap easily and the leaves and petals are crisp, usually one to three weeks.

TO GET THE most from your roses—whether they're fresh or dried—try some of these rose-arranging ideas.

- Roses are at their most fragrant when their blooms are one-quarter to one-third open, so don't wait until it's too late to cut them.

- Hybrid teas, if conditioned properly, will last up to a week as cut flowers. The heirloom roses, while very beautiful and fragrant, are more fragile and will last just a few days.

- For a wonderfully fragrant and long-lasting bouquet, arrange dried lavender and roses in a small basket of dried flowers.

- Add clusters of rose hips and pine cones to an evergreen wreath for an attractive Christmas decoration.

PRESERVING ROSES WITH YOUR MICROWAVE

Microwave oven drying with silica gel (a desiccant that resembles white sand) gives the freshest, most colorful preserved flower possible, other than freeze-drying. You can dry lots of flowers with a small amount of silica gel. The disadvantages are that you can only dry one or two flowers at a time and it can be difficult to judge the correct drying time.

1. Preheat silica gel in the microwave for 1 minute on high power.

2. Pour a 1-inch layer of the preheated gel in a small, deep, microwave-safe container or cardboard box. (Do not use the container for food preparation after using the silica gel.)

3. Place a rose with a 1-inch stem into the silica gel. Gently cover the flower with more silica gel.

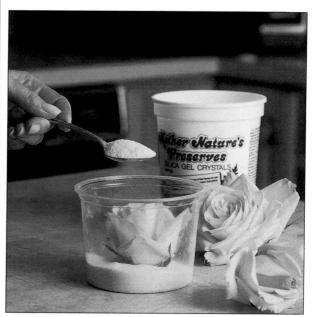

When you prepare roses for drying, gently sprinkle the silica gel over the rose, making sure to get it in between the rows of petals. Cover the rose entirely with the gel.

4. Microwave for 2 minutes on high power, using a turntable or rotating the container one-half turn every 30 seconds. Let the container cool for 20 to 30 seconds.

5. Carefully pour off the silica gel and check the condition of the flower. If it's too "done," cut the cooking time in half for the next rose.

6. Make a replacement stem with floral wire and floral wrapping tape. Insert a wire through the fat part of the flower just below the petals and center the wire. Gently bend the wire down on both sides and overlap the wire to form a single "stem."

7. Place the end of the floral tape against the rose and wrap the wires, twirling the wires and stretching the tape as you go. Tear off the tape at the base of the stem.

FUN FACT

THE ANCIENT ROMANS LOVED ROSES SO MUCH THEY CREATED GREENHOUSES HEATED WITH PIPED-IN HOT WATER FOR THE WINTER MONTHS IN ORDER TO HAVE YEAR-ROUND BLOOMS.

Use floral wire and floral tape to create a new stem for microwave-dried flowers. You need to gently stretch the tape as you wrap it onto the wire.

Your Seasonal Rose-Care Calendar

NOW THAT YOU KNOW the basics of good organic rose care, you need to know when to feed, mulch, water, plant, prune, and do all the other things roses need to thrive. Here's a calendar that gives you a glance of what you'll need to do each month throughout the year to keep your roses growing and blooming their best.

Also keep in mind that planting roses in Florida isn't the same as planting them in Maine because of the climatic conditions. That's why before you even start planning for roses, you need to know what hardiness zone you live in.

A plant's ability to withstand a given climate is called its hardiness. The USDA has developed a Plant Hardiness Zone Map that divides North America into ten numbered climatic zones. Zone 1 is the coldest, and Zone 10 is the warmest. Parts of Hawaii are even warmer and fall into Zone 11. You can check which zone you live in by looking at the map on page 106.

JANUARY

All climates:
- Plan your garden for the coming year, decide which roses you want to add, and order them.
- Purchase whatever new garden tools you need
- Clean, sharpen, and repair tools you have on hand.
- Check to make sure winter protection remains in place.

Zones 8 to 10: Plant both container-grown and bareroot roses and transplant any roses you want moved.

FEBRUARY

All climates: Clean, sharpen, and repair any equipment you didn't get to in January.

Zones 7 to 10: Plant container-grown and bareroot roses, and transplant roses as necessary.

MARCH

Zones 2 to 5:
- Make any adjustments to garden plans.
- Review information on roses you're planning to purchase.
- Order roses.

Zone 6: Remove winter protection from plants. Prune roses to shape, encourage new growth, or remove dead, diseased, or damaged wood.

Zones 7 to 10: Apply a balanced organic fertilizer to the soil around roses, scratching it in lightly.

APRIL

Zones 2 to 7:
- As soon as the soil is dry enough to work, plant bareroot and container-grown roses.
- Move any roses that would look better or grow better in another part of the garden.
- Prune roses to shape, to encourage new growth, or to remove dead, diseased, or damaged wood.

Zones 7 to 10:
- Remove faded flowers and remove buds on side blooms of hybrid teas for larger, longer-stemmed blooms.
- Plant container-grown roses.
- Apply balanced organic fertilizer to the soil and scratch in around roses.

Winter   **Spring**   **Summer**   **Fall**

MAY

 All climates: Check for pest and disease problems and water as necessary. Apply a balanced, organic fertilizer to the soil around roses. Gather roses for bouquets for yourself and friends.

Zones 2 to 4: Plant bareroot roses as weather and soil conditions permit.

JUNE

All climates:

- Remove faded flowers and remove buds on side blooms of cutting roses.

- Continue to check for pest and disease problems and control them as necessary.

- As rose canes extend themselves, tie and peg climbers to their structures.

- Enjoy your roses!

JULY

All climates:

- Continue to remove faded flowers, monitor for pests and disease problems, and water as necessary.

- Apply a foliar feeding of fish emulsion or liquid seaweed.

- Apply balanced organic fertilizer to the soil and scratch in around roses.

AUGUST

 All climates:

- Monitor for pests and disease and water as necessary.

- If desired, make a final application of a balanced fertilizer.

- Remove faded flowers and disbud side blooms on hybrid teas for larger, longer-stemmed blooms.

SEPTEMBER

Zones 2 to 6: Get new beds ready for spring planting. Stop removing faded flowers.

Zones 6 to 10: Send off orders for fall planting. Plant container-grown roses. Continue to keep garden areas weeded, and water as necessary.

OCTOBER

 All climates: Plan new plantings.

Zones 2 to 4:

- Prune roses.

- Remove leaves from plants

and from surrounding soil, and destroy.

- Apply winter mulch.

Zones 7 to 10: Send off orders for fall planting. Stop removing faded flowers.

NOVEMBER

 All climates: Send off your rose orders for spring planting.

Zones 5 to 7:

- Prune roses.

- Remove diseased leaves and canes from plants and from surrounding soil, and destroy.

- Apply winter mulch.

Zones 6 to 10: Get new beds ready for spring planting. Stop watering.

DECEMBER

All climates: Use disgarded Christmas tree branches as mulch around roses.

Zones 7 to 10:

- Plant container-grown and bareroot roses as weather and soil permit.

- Transplant roses as desired.

- Continue to check for pests and diseases.

Rose Glossary

Now that we've taken the mystery out of growing beautiful, healthy roses the organic way, you'll find it even easier to "talk roses" at garden centers and with your neighbors and gardening friends if you know the language. Or use this glossary to brush up on rose vocabulary that you might come across in catalogs or on nursery tags.

Alfalfa meal. One of the most commonly recommended organic fertilizers for roses.

Aphids. Soft-bodied green, red, pink, brown, or black insects about 1/8 inch long that attack roses. Found mostly on new growth, clustered on leaf tips and buds.

Axil. The angle between the cane and the upper surface of the leaf stalk.

Bareroot. A common form of shipping roses, where dormant roses are packed without pot or soil.

Beetles. Chewing insects with hard wings that eat rose leaves and flowers. Some larvae feed on the rose's roots.

Black spot. A fungal infection that forms black circles with yellow margins on leaves.

Bloodmeal. Also known as dried blood, bloodmeal is an animal by-product that contains 13 percent nitrogen. Sprinkled on garden beds, bloodmeal can repel rabbits.

Bonemeal. Finely ground bones (another animal by-product) that contains 10 to 12 percent phosphorus, 24 percent calcium, and a small amount of nitrogen.

Bud. A growth bud, or eye, found on a cane; a vegetative growing point located where a leaf joins the stem.

Bud union. The swollen point where the bud is joined with the rootstock.

Cane. A main stem, or basal shoot, of a rose, usually arising at or very near the bud union.

Clay soil. Soil that is made up of very fine particles that hold nutrients well but are poorly drained and difficult to work.

Climber. A rose that grows very tall and can be trained to grow on a trellis, an arbor, a pergola, or a wall.

Compost. Decomposed and partially decomposed organic matter that is dark in color and crumbly in texture. Used as a soil amendment, compost increases the water-holding capacity of sandy soil, improves drainage of clay soil, and is an excellent nutrient source for microorganisms, which later release nutrients to your plants.

Crown. The point on the rose where the canes sprout from the bud union.

Cultivar. Short for "cultivated variety," a cultivar is any plant that is bred for specific characteristics such as color, fragrance, disease resistance, or other desirable qualities.

Double flower. A rose that has 30 to 39 petals in four or more rows.

Eye (bud eye). A vegetative bud, or growing point, on a stem.

Feeder roots. Thin, fine-textured roots that absorb nutrients and water from the soil; also called hair roots.

Fertilizer. A natural or manufactured material that supplies one or more of the major nutrients—nitrogen (N), phosphorus (P), and potassium (K)—to growing plants.

Floribunda. Bushy roses that are a cross of hybrid tea and polyantha roses. Flowers may be single, semidouble, or double, and plants stand 2 to 4 feet tall.

Grafting. The process of joining a stem or bud of one cultivar onto the rooted stem, called the rootstock, of another cultivar.

Grandiflora. A cross of hybrid teas and floribunda roses that grow 4 to 6 feet tall. Flowers have high centers and are borne singly or in clusters.

Hip. The fruit or seedpod of the rose. Some roses have very showy hips, which add color and beauty to the fall and winter landscape.

Hybrid tea. Narrow, upright bushes that grow 3 to 5 feet high and need extra fertilizer to sustain heavy blooming. Flowers are long, narrow, and high-centered.

Lateral cane (branch). A side branch arising from a main, or basal, cane. Rambler roses, for instance, bloom on the lateral canes.

Leaf/leaflet. A rose leaf is compound and has three or more leaflets that make up the true leaf.

Loam. Textural class of soil that contains a balance of fine clay, medium-size silt, and coarse sand particles. Loam is easily tilled and retains moisture and nutrients effectively.

Main shoot. A basal or strong lateral cane.

Micronutrient. A plant nutrient needed in very small quantities, including copper, chlorine, zinc, iron, manganese, boron, and molybdenum.

Miniature rose. A rose that grows only 6 inches to 2 feet tall and all parts are miniaturized. The flowers can be single, semidouble, or double.

Modern rose. Any rose cultivar that was bred and introduced after 1867, the time when modern hybrid tea roses were first introduced.

Mosaic virus. A virus that causes leaves to develop circles of yellow or chartreuse, become streaked or mottled, or develop yellow netting. Plants may be stunted.

Mulch. A layer of an organic or inorganic material, such as shredded leaves, straw, bark, pine needles, lawn clippings, or black plastic, which is spread around plants to conserve soil moisture and discourage weeds. As organic mulches decompose, they help to build the soil.

New wood. A cane of the current year's growth. Some roses bloom only on new wood, while others bloom on the previous year's growth.

Old roses. Roses that were bred before 1867, the time when the modern hybrid tea rose was first introduced.

Old wood. A cane of the previous year's growth or older.

Own-root roses. Roses grown from cuttings, rather than being budded onto a rootstock of another plant.

Polyantha. Bushy, 2-foot plants that have narrow, finely textured leaves. Flowers are small and are borne in clusters.

Powdery mildew. A fungal disease that attacks new growth and flower buds, covering them with a thin, white, powdery substance. Growth becomes deformed.

Rambler. Similar to climbing roses, ramblers can be trained to grow on fences. They are once-blooming roses, and flowers are borne on new growth, so they must be pruned back severely each year to produce flowers the following summer.

Reversion. Suckers from the rootstock choking out or taking over from the growth of the bud graft.

Rootstock. The host plant or root portion (understock) onto which a bud of another type of rose is grafted.

Rust. A fungal disease that appears in spring as small orange spots on undersides of leaves and light yellow spots on the upper sides. Spots may also appear on canes. Most common on the Pacific Coast.

Sandy soil. Soil that contains more than 70 percent sand and less than 15 percent clay, generally easy to work and well drained but with poor nutrient- and water-holding abilities.

Scion. The technical term for the bud grafted onto a rootstock.

Semidouble flower. A flower that has 8 to 20 petals in two or three rows.

Shrub rose. A hardy, easy-to-grow plant that can grow as tall as 12 feet. The flowers can be single, semidouble, or double.

Silt. Refers to a soil particle of moderate size—larger than clay but not as large as sand.

Single flower. A flower with 5 to 7 petals in a single row.

Soil amendment. A material added to the soil to make it more productive by improving its structure, drainage, or aeration.

Soil pH. A number from 1 to 14 that is a measure of the acidity or alkalinity of soil, with 7 indicating neutrality; below 7, acidity; and above 7, alkalinity. The pH of your soil has a great effect on what nutrients are available to your plants.

Soil structure. The physical arrangement of soil particles and interconnected pore spaces. Soil structure can be improved by the addition of organic matter. Walking on or tilling wet soil can destroy the soil aggregates and ruin the soil's structure.

Soil texture. The proportions of sand, silt, and clay in a particular soil.

Species rose. Any rose that occurs naturally in nature. There are over 200 species of roses from which all other types of roses are bred.

Standard. Also called a tree rose, a standard is a rose that is grafted to a stalk (or standard), which in turn is grafted to rootstock, meaning there are two bud unions on a standard rose. These roses can be planted in the ground or used in containers as accent plants.

Stem. A branch of a cane, which emerges from a bud eye and bears leaves and at least one flower.

Sucker. A growing stem that arises from a rootstock below the bud union.

Thorn. The prickle, or sharp spine, found on the stem of roses.

Understock. The base of the plant, providing the root system, onto which the scion or bud of another rose is grafted; also called the rootstock.

Recommended Reading & Resources

Books & Periodicals

Browne, Jim, et. al. *Rose Gardening—The American Garden Guides*. NY: Pantheon Books, Knopf Publishing Group, 1995.

Druitt, Liz. *The Organic Rose Garden.* Dallas, TX: Taylor Publishing, 1996.

Green, Douglas. *Tender Roses for Tough Climates*. Shelburne, VT: Chapters Publishing, Ltd., 1997.

Martin, Clair G., et. al. *100 English Roses for the American Garden*. NY: Workman Publishing, 1997.

McKeon, Judith C. *The Encyclopedia of Roses*. Emmaus, PA: Rodale, 1995.

Oster, Maggie. *The Rose Book*. Emmaus, PA: Rodale, 1994.

Parker, Helen, editor. *Eyewitness Garden Handbooks—Roses*. London: Dorling Kindersley, 1996.

Scanniello, Stephen, editor. *Easy-Care Roses: Low-Maintenance Charmers*. Brooklyn, NY: Brooklyn Botanic Garden, 1995.

Schneider, Peter. *Taylor's Guide to Roses.* Rev. ed. NY: Houghton Mifflin, 1995.

Welch, William C. *Antique Roses for the South*. Dallas, TX: Taylor Publishing, 1990.

Rose Sources

Antique Rose Emporium
Route 5, Box 143
Brenham, TX 77833
Phone: (409) 836-9051
      (800) 441-0002
Fax: (409) 836-0928
Own-root, bareroot, and container roses; old world and shrub roses; also some hybrid teas and others

Edmunds' Roses
6235 SW Kahle Road
Wilsonville, OR 97070
Phone: (888) 481-7673
Fax: (503) 682-1275
E-mail: edmunds@edmundsroses.com
Web site: www.edmundsroses.com
Modern hybrid teas, grandifloras, and floribundas; climbing and shrub roses

Forestfarm
990 Tetherow Road
Williams, OR 97544-9599
Phone: (541) 846-7269
Web site: www.forsetfarm.com
Species roses and other own-root varieties

Greenmantle Nursery
3010 Ettersburg Road
Garberville, CA 95542
Phone: (707) 986-7504
Organically grown own-root roses

Heirloom Old Garden Roses
24062 NE Riverside Drive
St. Paul, OR 97137
Phone: (503) 538-1576
Own-root old roses and David Austin roses

Jackson & Perkins
One Rose Lane
P.O. Box 1028
Medford, OR 97501
Phone: (800) 872-7673
        (800) 292-4769
Fax: (800) 242-0329
E-mail: webmaster@jackson-perkins.com
Web site: www.jackson-perkins.com
*Grafted hybrid teas and modern roses; some
Austin and Rugosa roses*

Michael's Premier Roses
9759 Elder Creek Road
Sacramento, CA 95829
Phone: (916) 369-ROSE
Fax: (916) 361-1141
E-mail: michael@michaelsrose.com
Web site: www.michaelsrose.com
*Many varieties of miniature, modern, and
other roses*

The Mini-Rose Garden
P.O. Box 203
Cross Hill, SC 29332
Phone: (888) 998-2424
Fax: (864) 998-4947
E-mail: minirose@ais-gwd.com
Web site: www.minirose.ais-gwd.com
Miniature roses

Nor'East Miniature Roses, Inc.
P.O. Box 307
58 Hammond Street
Rowley, MA 01969
Phone: (800) 426-6485
Fax: (978) 948-5487
E-mail: nemr@shore.net
Web site: www.noreast-miniroses.com
Miniature roses

The Roseraie at Bayfields
P.O. Box R(wb)
Waldoboro, ME 04572
Phone: (207) 832-6330
Fax: (800) 933-4508
E-mail: zapas@roseraie.com
Web site: www.roseraie.com
Old-world and modern shrub roses

The Rose Ranch
P.O. Box 10087
Salinas, CA 93912
Phone: (408) 758-6965
Own-root old and rare roses

Roses Unlimited
Route 1, Box 587
North Deer Wood Drive
Laurens, SC 29360
Phone: (864) 682-7673
Fax: (864) 682-2455
E-mail: rosesunlmt@aol.com
Web site: http://members.aol.com/
        rosesunlmt/index.html
*Many varieties of own-root roses, species
roses, old garden roses, English roses, and
hybrid teas*

Vintage Gardens
2833 Old Gravenstein Highway South
Sebastopol, CA 95472
Phone: (707) 829-2035
Fax: (707) 829-9516
Web site: www.vintagegardens.com
Many varieties of antique and other roses

Wayside Gardens
1 Garden Lane
Hodges, SC 29695
Phone: (800) 845-1124
Fax: (800) 457-9712
E-mail: orders@waysidegardens.com
Web site: www.waysidegardens.com
*Old world and Austin roses, hybrid teas,
floribundas, and shrub roses*

Yesterday
802 Brown's Valley Road
Watsonville, CA 95076
Phone: (831) 728-1901
E-mail: postmaster@rosesofyesterday.com
Web site: www.rosesofyesterday.com
Many varieties of old and new roses

Acknowledgments

Contributors to this book include Maggie Oster (from *The Rose Book,* Rodale, 1994) and Sarah Wolfgang Heffner. Thanks also to Melissa Bennett for letting me cut her last roses of summer for the photographs on pages 28, 87, and 88.

Photo Credits

Matthew Benson 36, 39, 43 (top), 46 (top), 50, 56, 60, 61 (bottom), 64

Rob Cardillo 30, 53 (middle and bottom), 54 (top and middle), 94, 95

Crandall & Crandall 67 (bottom), 68 (bottom), 69

Dembinsky Photo Associates 68 (top), 83

Daniel D'Agostini 45

Saxon Holt i, 2, 4, 6, 8, 9, 10, 11, 12, 13, 14, 15, 20 (bottom), 22, 27, 41, 42, 46 (bottom), 47, 55, 72, 73 (bottom), 74, 76, 77, 78, 79, 84, 89, 90

Impact Marketing 91

Kit Latham 75, 82

Andrew Lawson 20 (top), 73 (top)

Holly Lynton 43 (bottom)

Allan Mandell 5

Mitch Mandel 31, 32, 53 (top), 54 (bottom)

J. Paul Moore 18, 70

John Peden vi, 21

Maria Rodale iv

Richard Shiell 3 (top), 17, 19, 23, 24, 25, 26, 33, 38, 39

Rick Wetherbee 3 (bottom), 34, 35, 44, 48, 49, 52, 59, 61 (top), 62, 66, 67 (top), 81, 86

Kurt Wilson 28, 57, 87, 88, 92, 93

Index

USDA Plant Hardiness Zone Map

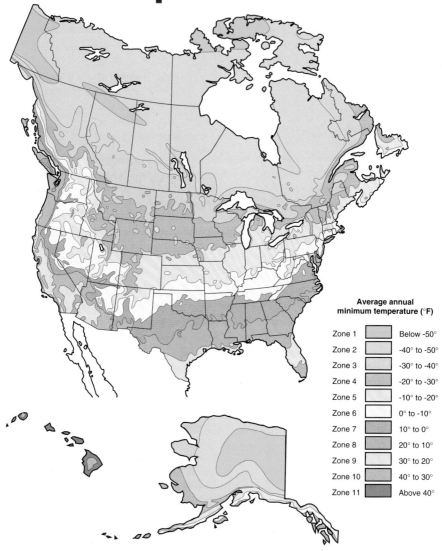

Average annual minimum temperature (°F)

Zone		Temperature
Zone 1		Below -50°
Zone 2		-40° to -50°
Zone 3		-30° to -40°
Zone 4		-20° to -30°
Zone 5		-10° to -20°
Zone 6		0° to -10°
Zone 7		10° to 0°
Zone 8		20° to 10°
Zone 9		30° to 20°
Zone 10		40° to 30°
Zone 11		Above 40°

This map was revised in 1990 and is recognized as the best indicator of minimum temperatures available. Look at the map to find your area, then match its color to the key at the right. When you've found your color, the key will tell you what hardiness zone you live in. Remember that the map is a general guide; your particular conditions may vary.